WAYNE ANTHONY

CLASS OF 88

Find the warehouse.
Lose the hitmen.
Pump the beats.

1 3 5 7 9 10 8 6 4 2

Virgin Books, an imprint of Ebury Publishing,
20 Vauxhall Bridge Road,
London SW1V 2SA

Virgin Books is part of the Penguin Random House group
of companies whose addresses can be found at
global.penguinrandomhouse.com

Penguin
Random House
UK

First published in the United Kingdom by Virgin Books in 1998
This updated edition published by Virgin Books in 2018

www.penguin.co.uk

A CIP catalogue record for this book is available
from the British Library

ISBN 9780753552124

Typeset in 11/17.25 pt Sabon
by Integra Software Services Pvt. Ltd, Pondicherry

Printed and bound in Great Britain by Clays Ltd, St Ives PLC

Penguin Random House is committed to a sustainable future
for our business, our readers and our planet. This book is
made from Forest Stewardship Council® certified paper.

Contents

'I see, said the blind man, without any eyes'

Bernice Orenthia Rookwood
July 4 1911–February 25 1997

Bless their cottons

Mom – even if I wrote 100,000 words about my emotions for you and my family, who have stood by me through thick and thin, I couldn't do you justice. The same is true of my sisters Teena, Nichola and Bianca, who deserve nothing but the best. My dad Claude *(ar me this)*. My stepdad Colin, nephew Cain and the rest of my family. Ian Gittins and the team at Virgin for publishing this work in spite of current media hyperbole and allowing their first-time author full freedom of expression: you have reinforced my belief that anything is possible. Keith and KP, without whom Genesis may never have existed. DJ Dominic (spread love) and Darren (Soul Café, Tenerife). Cheers for the use of your computer, printer and paper.

Knowledge is power.

RIP: Gurkan, Paul Rowe and Micky Mif.

Warning

My intention in this book isn't to glamorise drug use but to chronicle a change in people's attitudes. Life doesn't revolve around drugs: it revolves around society. I'm not advising anybody to take Ecstasy or any other class-A substance. Users know the dangers. To pop pills is to play Russian roulette with your mind and body. Nowadays, mass-produced tablets contain all kinds of shit. Nobody really knows what they're taking, and this can result in otherwise healthy people dying of chemically induced illnesses. This story serves as a social record of England in the late Eighties. Before you pass judgement, read on without prejudice.

Wayne Anthony

Introduction

I have no idea how many times in the last 30 years someone has said to me, 'I wish I had a time machine.' They could choose any period in history, but no, it's back to the glory days of Acid House.

A whole generation of people – my generation – have grown old, gracefully or disgracefully, shaped by the life-changing experiences we enjoyed together between 1987 and 1990. When I look into a mirror now, the laughter lines tell their own story but, if I am honest, Acid House still feels like yesterday.

I still see the world the same way as I did three decades ago – minus, of course, the MDMA, flashing lights and packed warehouses! If somebody had told me when I took my first yellow pill that I would go on to stage some of the biggest illegal parties in the country, I would never have believed them. I had never arranged so much as a birthday party before the first Genesis in '88.

When I first sat down to write *Class of 88* in 1996, I had no idea whether it would ever see the light of day. In all honesty, I wasn't even sure I was up to the task. My English is average at best, and I had never written more than four or five pages in my life. Yet as soon as I put pen to paper, it all made sense.

When I think back to Genesis '88, I feel a great sense of pride. We pushed our boundaries way beyond what we thought they were. There were so many high points. Standing among thousands of people after a magical mystery tour around the South East's motorway system. Climbing fences, running over railway tracks and rowing boats across canals to reach the secret party locations. Counting large black bags of cash in a back room of a dirty warehouse had its moments as well.

We were tearing down emotional barriers and building new bridges. House music was the catalyst and MDMA the accelerator.

Acid House is 30 years old now – far older than me and my partners, Keith Brooks and Andrew Pritchard, were when we started our adventure in '87. We were just 22: three lads from Hackney. Our manor was going through hard times, and to be honest, a lot of people we knew were used to nicking stuff out of warehouses, not taking equipment in!

Yet there we were, the three of us, bolt-croppers in our hands, breaking open doors, embracing the future. If the police turned up when the party was on – and they usually did – I'd pretend to be George Michael's manager, or from EMI or Channel 4. It was too exciting to worry or feel frightened.

The fear came later. Our efforts got noticed by the kind of organised criminal gangs who usually rob Post Offices or banks at gunpoint. They read in the media that we could earn half a million quid in one night – but in truth, we were just kids, off our heads on love drugs, holding hands and cuddling each other.

When the gangsters showed up, I found myself strapped to a chair with a hood over my head, cold shotgun barrels against my temple. Organised criminals and Yardie gangs made hay in our lawless, loved-up zones. When three gun-toting Yardies came to rob one of our parties in North London in '89, it was like a scene from *Reservoir Dogs*.

Of course, ravers had no idea that behind the scenes, party promoters were being robbed, kidnapped or worse. Why would they know? The double life got so stressful that I often found solace in Class A drugs. It helped to blur the lines.

Yet the grief was worth it. The most uplifting part of the entire journey was the togetherness of strangers and seeing people coming together and opening their hearts up to love. It might sound corny, but this is my personal experience. It's the sort of thing that only comes along once in a lifetime, and you never forget it.

I'm proud of the Genesis crew and the fact we worked side by side and broke into warehouses with Sunrise,

Energy, Biology and a few others. I'm also incredibly proud of *Class of 88*. When I see copies of the original book changing hands on the internet, it means a lot. It also means that it is worth bringing it out again so more people can read our crazy story.

At the end of the first book, 20 years ago, I looked back at my (mis)adventures and asked myself: 'Would I do it all again?' I answered: 'No fucking chance!' Now, I think I spoke too soon. If a time machine could take me back to 1987, I would be on it like a shot.

What is the biggest thing that Acid House and being part of the class of '88 taught me? When humanity dreams big, we can move mountains.

Wayne Anthony, 2018, still loved up and game …

A Hitchhiker's Guide to Dance Party Organisations

Acid House was Made on Earth from the ashes of an Apocalypse Now in a time of Sin, Hedonism and Dance with the Devil. I was standing in The Attic near Curtain Road experiencing The Living Dream. I took the Kaleidoscope from my jet-pack and gazed across the Mutoid Wasteground at Trip City. There she stood in her natural Raw beauty: a Pyramid of Knowledge, a Palace where even Kings and Queens can seek Asylum. An inspiring Loud Noise echoed into the night sky. A Brainstorm took shape. The Project was to travel hundreds of light years away to the period of 2000 AD. The entire human race was High on Hope of recovering the Delirium water decontamination formula. The Future of Planet Westworld depended on the accomplishment of this mission. My journey through the Labyrinth of Dungeons across the Common south of the river was about to be rewarded by seeing the Sunrise for the very first time. With **Adrenaline** rushing through my veins I immediately felt the **Energy** and **Atmosphere** of a **New Generation** at the peak of an original **World Dance.** The air force was based on **The Doo at the Zoo,** where several rocket ships took flight, bound for the **Land of Oz.** Their **Trip** was to go **Back to the Future** and, **In Search of Space** on a **Magical Mystery Tour,** seek the key to enlightenment and **Humanity. Shoom!** A **Space** shuttle flew over **The Rave at the Cave.** The **Mad** professors who were **Beyond Therapy** stood guard by the stargate to **Infinity.** They had all the questions but not the answers; the geniuses were banished to the **Planet MFI** but had somehow escaped. There were people wandering the streets in **Shock** and suffering **Amnesia;** they arrived from **Pacha** and were gathering in the square outside **The Mud Club.** There is only one tribe that truly knows **The Meaning of Life:** the **We Generation,** children of the fifth sun. The **Slaughter House** of **Hypnosis** and **Confusion** was transformed into a **Hacienda** of complete **Bliss** and **Tranquillity.** The **Unit 4** in **Pasha** on **Clink Street** was reserved for the **Fridge;** this was the **Academy** and **Center-Force** of our **Fantasy. The Ratpack** was asked to search the **Spectrum** of **Organised Kaos,** whilst the **Rage** of the **Heaven** altered the **Biology** state of **Boys Own.** Their destination was the **Loft** of the well-known **Car Wash** in **Weekend World,** for a midnight data **Raid. The Fantastic Ibiza** is said to be a richly deserved **Wonderland.** Before we make that important journey we have to look back and reflect on an era when People Power **Run Tings.** A time when **Eco-Warriors** did battle with invading forces and won. **RIP** negative thoughts and **Phantasy** as we are transported along life's super highway into an oasis of **Genesis.**

PART ONE

Profound Joy

A NEW BEGINNING

Remember the days when authors began their novels with 'Once upon a time'? They were cool dudes, man. They wrote stories of love, passion, fantasy and obsession – but times, people and traditions change. People have to face up to the harsh realities of everyday life, and reality has many faces.

This story is about reality and a drug invented over fifty years ago that has inspired heightened awareness in people and allowed them to free their emotions. I vaguely remember nine or ten years before 1988's Summer Of Love, back in the days when everybody would be posing and drinking in wine bars and clubs like Browns around London. The musical vibe back then was soul, funk and pop.

In those early Eighties days there might be 500 people in a club but they'd all be in their own separate groups. Nobody ventured out to meet anyone new except for people of the opposite sex. Gangs of youths would go out, giving it loads, drinking loads, then having a tear-up. This was regarded as the norm: we'll fight them on the beaches, terraces and in the clubs and pubs. Every Saturday, England became a battleground as home-team supporters clashed with visitors. It was a time of discontent, boredom, frustration and no direction.

Nobody thought about change: this was all they knew. Me and my mates used to spend the evenings in 1987 and early '88 drinking in a pub in Hackney almost every night. My crowd were all proper people: salt of the earth who came from all different backgrounds and knew how to earn a pound note. Blaggers, roofers, hoisters, forgers, growlers and fighters. You name it, they done it; except for muggings, bag snatching, anything to do with kids or abusing women. We were all good mates who looked out for one another.

The music in our local was mainly pop, and guest disco DJs played their own dated sets. It wasn't a particularly nice pub but the attraction was knowing some of your pals would always be there. Our group was tight and together, but nobody would express any emotion beyond 'You know I'll back you up any day, mate.' You didn't walk up to your pal and say 'I love you, bruv' with a hug and a kiss on the cheek. You'd soon be knocked on the deck, with no mates.

Most people in London supported Tottenham, Arsenal, Chelsea, West Ham, QPR or Millwall. Violence was the only way of letting frustrations rip. Our crew were into money so we knocked football fights on the head. There was north, south, east, and west London against each other as well as battles between northerners and southerners. Fights in pubs and clubs were going off all the time and the part of town you came from was high on the list of reasons to get you a beating if you ever ventured out of your own patch.

The recession was in full bloom and bad attitudes filled the air. In 1988 there were all kinds of insane happenings around the world. Everlasting wars, environmental erosion, starvation, racial tension and extreme prejudice were just a few of the globe's problems. There was a cultural agenda of hard-headed, selfish values and the borders between different races and cultures were growing ever higher.

Of course, Ecstasy brought about a dramatic change. Thinking back to that first rush and trying to describe it to someone who hasn't experienced taking E isn't easy. You'd introduce yourself to everyone who walked past you, with a big smile and arms stretched out wide to give them a hug. They were your brothers and sisters and it didn't matter how you looked, dressed or danced. Nobody cared: we were all one. Integration accelerated to a new level, a new understanding, a new beginning.

I'd taken my first ever Ecstasy, like a lot of people, in Ibiza in 1987, but in all honesty it must have been a duff tab because it didn't have much effect on me. I was always much more into charlie, anyway. Then one night in London during the summer of '88 I was taken to Heaven, a club next to Charing Cross station, and was blown away. Just half a tablet I was given by a friend made me feel euphoric, elated and like a fresh, very alive person, and I was uplifted by the cool vibe and positive energy being given out by everybody in the gaff. This was something new, something special. I knew it could change my life, and I knew I wanted in.

I was still talking about my night at Heaven to my pals down the pub in Hackney a few days later. However, none of them cared or had any interest in coming with me the following week. They just issued dire warnings about what they'd do to any geezers who ever tried to put their arms around them the way blokes at Heaven had been doing. Even Keith, my oldest mate in the world, wasn't at all interested in coming with me.

I simply couldn't wait to go back to Heaven and I started telephoning other pals to see if they'd heard of this fantastic club. I was in luck. Some local friends of mine went out almost every night and told me to meet up with them on Friday and go to Camden Palace in north London. I became very excited at the prospect of taking a proper, whole E.

Friday night came: Party Time! I met up with a few lads I knew well including Gary, Michael, Owen and

Gurkan, who are a couple of years younger than me but totally up for it. These boys had been going out since day one so they knew all the ropes. We dropped a pill fifteen minutes before getting in the motor and making our way to Camden. The track 'Break for Love' was playing at maximum volume and we started singing: 'I'll be there in the morning, baby, to hold you tight, and that's why, baby, you don't have to wonder why, why I love you. Break, break for love!'

I felt the E coming on and my heart was beating faster and my whole body felt lighter. By the time we reached the Palace we were all buzzing: wheeeeeeeeyyyyyyy! What a feeling! There was a major queue around the building, which reached into the street behind, but we headed for the front and joined the queue near the main entrance. As long as the doorman didn't see you nobody really complained; it was such a long queue that people didn't mind if you politely pushed in.

Ten minutes later and, after a class-A search, we were in the club. We walked along a corridor and ended up on a balcony, overlooking the packed dance floor and a raised theatre stage. Behind us were several tiered floors, with tables and chairs, which went right up to the top of the building. We went down a staircase that ran down the middle of the balcony to the ground floor. There was also a bar that ran the length of the back wall.

Camden Palace holds 3,000 people and tonight it was so rammed that we could hardly move. A group of around 300 enthusiastic clubbers by one staircase were going for it big time, waving their arms in the air as if they were demented. The DJ was playing 'Salsa House' by Richie Rich and now and then he'd talk into a mike hooked up to the PA system.

'This one's for the Ecstasy posse!' the DJ yelled.

Everybody in one corner began shouting, 'Ecstasy, Ecstasy, Ecstasy!'

We joined them and shouted out loud, 'Ecstasy, Ecstasy, Ecstasy!'

Some punters glared at us, wondering what the fuck we were going on about. Most of the punters were very smart-casual but us lot were in smiley T-shirts, bandanas, ripped jeans, ponchos, African robes, oversized jumpers, dungarees, straw hats and Timberlands with laces undone. This was our uniform and we wore it with pride.

My rush was peaking and I felt huge energy and love for the people around me. I looked over the hundreds of bopping heads cramming the dance floor, directly at the DJ on the main stage. A laser clicked on and created a giant blue time tunnel. The smoke machine gave the vision a surreal edge and I stood staring at it for a while. Another world beyond this huge vortex beckoned me to its shores. My body twitched nervously until my astral projection began to rise from my body and my transparent spirit looked down at me, looking back at him.

I viewed the images from both angles and felt as though I had two minds, both evaluating the situation. Leaving my physical body, the astral projection started slowly gliding above the heads of 1,000 party animals towards this fascinating doorway to another dimension. Although the spirit was in real time, an eerie silence engulfed the dome. Footsteps echoed loudly as I walked across air whilst preparing to enter a future or a past ... then hands raised in the air broke the smooth surface of the laser walls.

A familiar voice called my name and I felt the sound of blood rushing through my veins: russsssssshhhhh.

'Oi oi, you OK, mate? Drink some water and sit down for a minute. It'll pass soon, don't worry.'

'I feel really sick,' I groaned.

'Just try to hold it together as long as you can, but if you're sick you'll feel a lot better.'

My jawbone was shaking rapidly, making my teeth clatter. The noise vibrated throughout my body; this powerful effect was unlike anything I'd experienced before. My whole body felt light and my mind felt intensely stimulated. The bad feeling soon passed, and in no time I was wandering around the club smiling at everyone.

You could tell the people who were on E: they'd come up and give you a hug. The other punters just looked at us as if we were mad, or gay. But no one gave a shite what anyone else thought, or if it put a black mark against their credibility. If judgement was passed on the merit of my behaviour and the sight of a big yellow smiley-face T-shirt, it wasn't my problem. Right now the only emotion I could feel or express was love. Four hours flew past and I found myself back with the Ecstasy posse, having happily met a bucketload of new friends. My rush had stabilised but my energy levels were still surprisingly high.

All my mates were shouting, screaming at the tops of their voices, 'Get right on one, matey, get right on one, matey!'

One guy walked straight up to me who resembled a Shoomer and was dressed in flares, knitted jumper and Converse boots. His jawbone was all over the gaff and with an accent that was pure Eton, he said, 'Are you E-ing?'

I fell about laughing. 'E-ing? I'm off my nut, mate!'

We shook hands and he shuffled over to someone else, asking the same question: 'Are you E-ing?'

The DJ was on a roll and each track he played was greeted by loud applause. 'It Takes Two', 'Sharp as a Knife', 'Dream Girl', 'Snappiness' and 'The Dance' were all part of his wicked set. The end of the night came in a flash. The DJ played his last track, which apparently he always spun at the end of his set every week.

Three thousand people were singing 'Ain't nobody loves me better, makes me happy, makes me feel this way' by Chaka Khan, Chaka Khan, Chaka Chaka Chaka Khan. It was 3.30 a.m. We drove back to our manor with music blaring and heads bopping. I was dropped off home and hugged each of my friends before disappearing into the house. I was starting to feel tired so went straight to bed. I had the best sleep for ages. When I awoke in the afternoon I felt totally refreshed and ready for the night ahead.

Saturday came to mean Sin at the Astoria on Tottenham Court Road, so the next night the lads picked me up and off we went. Although we had been out the night before, we looked OK, considering. Our timetable for the night was to get pilled up first, go to Sin and then on to the Slaughter House.

Nicky Holloway hosted Sin, where the auditorium was split on to two levels: a ground floor and a huge balcony area. Outside was the now obligatory massive queue, which you virtually needed a telescope to see the end of. A crash barrier and a long piece of thick rope kept the bods at the head of the line in order. The queue-jumping trick at the Astoria was to wander casually around the corner, keeping one eye on the security and the other wide open for an opportunity to duck under the rope at the front. You'd do this two at a time and as the next lot came round they would slip in front of you.

Before we knew it we were behind the DJ, jumping up and down on the tables. This wasn't the same experience as Camden Palace. Here, it seemed as if everyone in the whole club was on Ecstasy. Everybody waved their hands in the air and began clapping in time with the music.

Five, four, three, two, one, blast off! Yellow tab down the hatch, fire in the hole, prepare for meltdown. The mere thought of having the same rush as I'd experienced hours before was sending shivers down my spine. I bumped into loads of my new-found friends and some of my old ones and we hugged, expressing our friendship and a bond that would never break.

Around fifty of us huddled together and started chanting 'Aceeed, Aceeed, Aceeed!' and the next minute the whole place was chanting it, giving us a huge rush. The upper circle of the theatre had tables and chairs around the entire balcony and everyone was dancing and going nuts on top of them. I was under the influence of E but the electric atmosphere was overwhelming and seemed to exceed the drug.

I stopped dancing for a moment to absorb this stimulating energy and glanced across the room and spotted some friends sitting near the front circle. Their body language told me they weren't fully in control. One mate, Kacy, was leaning over the balcony watching 1,000 or so people grooving on the dance floor. I watched him for five minutes before he climbed on to the rail and sat down. There was nothing to prevent him falling 30 feet to the ground.

I started pushing my way through the crowd, not taking my eyes off him for a second. To my complete horror he kept both hands on the rail and tried to put his foot down on what he thought was the floor. The only object within reach was a lighting can attached to the wall. He felt the fixture beneath his foot and went to step off. With only seconds to spare, someone spotted him and grabbed him just in time.

Kacy didn't even know what had happened. His eyes were almost closed and he was a total mess. I asked him if he realised somebody had just saved his life, but unfortunately he couldn't even understand what we were saying. When I called Kacy the next day, he was uneasy and in a state of disbelief.

The gang of us came out of the Astoria still buzzing and nobody wanted to go home. A crowd was building up outside the club and across the road near some water fountains. A car pulled up at the traffic lights, blasting out a new clubbed-up version of 'Sympathy For The Devil'. Everyone started dancing in the roads and on the pavements. People were jumping in the fountains and traffic was brought to a complete halt for about half an hour.

The crowd were going nuts, screaming 'Street party!' Charing Cross Road is one of London's busiest roads and the tailback of cars reached all the way to Trafalgar Square. People in convertibles were standing on the seats of their cars, waving their hands to the music, and other people were dancing in the traffic. For that brief moment it was People Power, a feeling of total freedom. This wasn't just some passing cultural fad: it was going to be huge. We got to the motors parked in nearby Denmark Street and flicked coins to see who was going to drive. After half an hour's wait for the drivers' rushes to stabilise, we were on our way.

The Slaughterhouse was an old warehouse in the Smithfield meat market. I don't know if it originally operated as an abattoir or was just given that name by the promoters. The streets around the party location were bursting with energy but we drove to the front of the building to discover the doors had been closed because the venue was filled to capacity.

The thousand-strong crew outside tried their hardest to gain entry but this just made matters worse. Buzzing or not, we weren't getting into that gig and so we ended up at a pal's gaff where we danced to loud music until 11 a.m.

GENESIS CHAPTER ONE

I'd never even thought about organising warehouse parties until one night at Spectrum. I was talking to the kind of new-found friend I'd been making a lot of: the sort you meet while you're off your nut and tell your life story to. Everybody called him KP and I'd only met him a few weeks previously.

'There's a lot of money to be earned,' KP said.

Until then I'd worked in the music industry, managing bands. The idea of a completely new project intrigued me and I agreed to think it over. 'What would we be called?' I asked.

'Something with depth and meaning,' he replied.

KP had limited experience from arranging a few small gigs in the past. He said it was just a matter of finding a deserted warehouse, printing 500 flyers and distributing them to clubbers we met whilst out painting the town red. He had all his own equipment, including a sound system, some lights and a box of wicked tunes. Costs could be kept to a minimum and amount to no more than a grand: drinks would be on a sale or return basis, flyers cost £80, the doorman would be my stepdad, the bar manager his sister Nikki, DJ Tony Wilson took £100 and KP or myself would be on the door taking the money. We were one big, happy, productive, family affair about to put the G into hard graft.

A title is very important when marketing new ideas, and has to be thought over very carefully before a final decision can be made. We didn't want to change our chosen banner at a later stage for any reason, so the name had to be right from the start. That night I brainstormed myself unconscious and into a deep sleep, but not before noting ten titles that really stood out and made my hair stand on end.

The favoured choice for me was Genesis, a beautiful word that I thought summarised the *Zeitgeist*. This was an era that was dramatically changing millions of lives the world over, a time of evolution and revolution in the mass consciousness, of non-violence and positive attitudes. The fact we became one of the pioneering companies who influenced the New Age gave me a greater high than drugs ever could. You could keep the Swinging Sixties and the warehouse parties of the early Eighties: 'Get right on one, matey!'

A logo was the next step, and it had to represent the feelings of our company and also an understanding of this new society. The long search for a simple solution ended with a picture of Zeus, the highest of the Greek gods. This wasn't an attempt to offend any religions or cultures – the face simply complemented the name perfectly and gave the title more strength, feeling and body.

Top of our agenda, then, was to find a suitable warehouse away from residential properties, because local people would be the first to call the Old Bill, and if Dibble turned up before the event started, we'd be fucked. Secrecy was of the utmost importance. We couldn't afford to tell anyone where the gig was. Nobody knew, not even the lighting and sound crews. Everything was on a need-to-know basis.

Why? Because news of venue locations travels fast in this game. If the site address were given out in advance it would mean people turning up too early at the venue instead of at the designated meeting points. This draws attention to the venue and, before you know it, disaster strikes: the Old Bill turns up in force and every piece of equipment in the gaff is confiscated.

Meeting points were strategic strong points when organising parties, and promoters took full advantage of these tactical positions. They couldn't be too close to the venue, because that made the Met's job of finding us far too easy. It had to be somewhere that most people could find without difficulty and somewhere with enough space for cars to park so as not to obstruct other road users.

One of our guys would be assigned the job of keeping this point under tight control and giving directions to anyone who asked. If they didn't ask, he wouldn't tell them. Veteran clubbers knew anyone found standing around the arranged meet had the venue details. The logic being that if you didn't know to ask the person the address, you must be the Old Bill. It was very simple, really.

Some friends had the keys to a small warehouse in Aldgate East. So KP and I went down to inspect the property and surrounding area at 1 o'clock on a cold and wet Tuesday morning. The entrance was near the corner of a very busy road so we had to be doubly careful not to be seen. The keys we'd been given didn't fit the main doors, so we walked around looking for a weak point of entry until we spotted an open balcony that ran inside the building and down some stairs to the front entrance. We scaled the wall and reached the balcony in no time and, seeing an open window, we climbed in.

The venue could hold about 300 people, with maybe another 50 on the balcony. There was loads of rubbish scattered about the place but nothing too bad. Even the main entry door could be unlocked from the inside. We didn't have to break into any part of the building, and so we left it exactly as we found it so as not to arouse suspicion. We'd found our site.

The flyer we'd had printed to our specifications contained the necessary party information. It would be no more than an ordinary flyer by today's standards, but back then it was one of the best I'd ever seen. Private Party laws meant flyers had to be printed as invites. The phrases 'No invite – no entry' and 'Over 18s only' had to feature prominently on all flyers.

As well as proclaiming our parties to be private events, this tactic was also a way of keeping certain undesirables at bay, from the Old Bill and dickheads to journalists. We only handed flyers out at specific clubs and parties where we figured anybody attending would be on the level.

Think back and remember that, in those days, there were no more than 5,000 party people and clubbers in the whole of England, and half of those were in Ibiza or Tenerife. Party details were spread by word of mouth, and back-handed flying: if you were there, then you must know someone who knew someone. One big happy family. If you didn't know someone's name, you knew their face.

The people who actually brought the invites to the doors of gigs were usually new to the scene. The veterans knew this was to cover ourselves within the law. Barring the geeks already mentioned, we'd let in anyone who didn't look dodgy. The ones who *did* fit the look of Dibble were astonished when they were refused entry. We don't have anything against the police – we just wanted our night to last as long as possible.

There was a club or house party on virtually every night and we personally went out and handed flyers to the type of people we wanted at our shindig. When giving someone a flyer we'd always say exactly what it was, e.g. 'Genesis, 10 December'. Our aim was to fix the name in people's minds as well as to promote the event. We got a fantastic response from everyone; they all loved the name and logo.

I remember feeling very nervous before our first night. The butterflies in my stomach were flapping like mad. We'd been out promoting our gig the night before, so we didn't get much sleep. This was what we'd been working our bollocks off for, what we'd been planning, and tonight was the night.

At the time I didn't personally know any other party organisers, so I didn't know if my panic attacks were normal or not. This was all completely new to me and I didn't know what to expect. I *did* know that it was extremely nerve-racking. One, we were in a building we shouldn't be in. Two, the police could arrive at any time and we'd get seriously chored. Three, if no one turned up we'd be very embarrassed. This event had to work or I would just lose faith and quit.

We entered the warehouse at approximately 5 p.m. on Saturday night. It was winter and felt like the dead of night. We were close to the City, which is very quiet at this time with hardly any traffic on the road. Once the venue was cleaned up and secured we called our van driver, who for security reasons had parked ten minutes away. Having a van outside the site wouldn't be a good idea because it had all the equipment in it, and if he got caught we'd be up shit creek without a sound system.

There are a lot of warehouses in the area so it's not that unusual to see a van being unloaded. Part of Petticoat Lane market runs along this road and opens on Sundays, and a few vans were scattered along the road anyway, but I didn't want to take the chance of parking ours there. The van pulled up outside and we quickly began loading its contents into the building, then began work on transforming a dirty warehouse into a state-of-the-art dance arena.

During the previous week we had visited an army surplus store and bought a carful of props, including giant snow nets, white and green camouflage nets and full-size parachutes still in their packs. We slogged our guts out setting the equipment up and then moved on to the props, which we pinned up to the ceiling and around the walls. We had three old still-projectors, which projected on to the chutes and nets and the venue looked like the interior of a futurist nightclub. It was the nuts, mate!

Even if the party flopped I knew by now that I would enjoy myself, and the visuals gave me a surreal feeling of warmth. A small room next to the one we were using made a great bar. We put a table across the doorway; the bar was operational.

The meeting point was set for 10 p.m. and I went to see if anyone had turned up. At ten to ten there wasn't a soul in sight – my bubble had burst. Twenty minutes later I returned and found fifteen cars parked with clubbers running from one car to another. They were in high spirits and really up for it, jumping on their cars and dancing in the street.

'Where's the party, mate?'

The most important ingredient, after the class As, is the music. KP had the tunes and we got a few of our pals to play a kicking party set of Balearic, New Beat and rock. The set featured tracks from artistes like Sure Beats Working, Flesh, The Thrashing Doves, Carly Simon and Prince, and was a refreshing break from Acid House. The combined effects of music, lights, smoke, strobes and Ecstasy brought on an incredible russsssh and everyone in the room waved their arms in the air and went fucking mental.

At midnight we had about 200 people in the warehouse but it didn't look like getting much busier. Then, as if on cue, loads of cars started pulling up outside, and we received news that the Rave At The Cave in south London had been raided. Based in an old mechanics, garage in the arches at Elephant and Castle, it could hold 2,000 people and was very popular.

Tonight the police had raided the gaff big time with video cameras, mobile strip-search units, sniffer dogs, news teams, the whole deal. Everyone in the place was strip-searched but only a few arrests were made, leaving hundreds of people pissing in the wind until they found out about our intimate gathering. My smile turned into a full Chelsea beamer as my levels of adrenaline went up a notch.

I had already dropped a Cali so I felt extremely happy with myself and the party. We squeezed as many people inside as possible – what a fantastic atmosphere. It was togetherness, a unified race towards a brighter future. I went around to almost everyone introducing myself and thanking them for coming. Kiss FM's Sarah HB, who was not a DJ at that point, was amongst the many revellers and so was Energy/World Dance's Anton Le Pirate, who was then not yet a party promoter.

When I first started promoting the event I had given invites to all the people I hung out with, but none of them had turned up. At about 4 a.m. they all made an appearance, having been elsewhere because they'd assumed my gig would be shit (cheers, lads!) My oldest friend, Keith, who I used to drink with, chase birds with and abuse class As with, couldn't believe how many people had come. I knew Keith wanted to be a part of the action by the way he was talking about it. We go back a long way so I wanted to bring him in anyway. KP didn't think we needed another partner but agreed to think about it.

Meanwhile, the party was in full swing. People were dancing everywhere and on top of anything that would hold their weight. At 5 a.m. a fire bell rang out from the warehouse next door where we had a look-out. Shit! That meant Dibble was on the way!

My stepfather was looking after the money for us; when the alarm went off we decided the money should be taken to a safe house. I ran upstairs along the balcony into the main room and to the bar, where by now Nikki was giving the drinks away free. I told her the score and we ran down the stairs to the front, gave her all the door cash, which she hid, and escorted her to the main entrance.

The police had arrived and shut off the electricity; sadly, the party was over. Everyone had to leave. We stepped into the street through a corridor of laughing policemen, who were taking the piss out of everyone. Bods with wobbling jaws were walking out bare-chested into the cold winter air, sweat and steam rising from their bodies.

'OK then, who's the organiser? Does anyone know who put this party on?' I heard a policeman ask as we slipped around the corner.

This was probably Dibble's first encounter with E'd-up party animals and I think they were quite surprised. None of us was stopped, so we met up at my place to have a count-up. We'd made two grand profit, which wasn't bundles but a fucking good start. We sat down and went over the night's events, still rushing from the pill swallowed earlier.

'So what do you reckon?' I was asked.

Well, after four weeks of attending different clubs and house parties, with very little sleep and popping untold pills, and having seen our party brought to a premature halt, and having had to abandon all our equipment behind, I still felt pretty pukka. The planning, lighting and sound production and music had all worked like a dream.

'I reckon we should have another party as soon as possible.'

We went back to the warehouse later that day to check if the stuff was still there. Luckily, every single item of equipment was still in place. We quickly and nervously loaded up the van and high-tailed it out at light-speed. On our way back to a small lock-up garage we had in Walthamstow, all we could talk about was finding another gaff to stage Genesis Chapter Two.

GENESIS CHAPTER TWO: THE STRUGGLE CONTINUES

We spent the following week searching for warehouses. Our search covered three industrial estates with no sign of a suitable venue. It was an easy enough procedure: when we spotted commercial-lease boards for prospective sites, we'd pull over and have a look through the windows.

Driving through the backstreets of Hackney a week earlier, we had seen reflections of disco lights through a warehouse window. Stopping by the entrance, we went inside to investigate. The spacious building was perfect and big enough to contain at least 4,500 people. Some geezers were gathered round a DJ console mounted on milk crates at the far end of the building. Music was playing quietly in the background whilst poxy lights on boxes strove to keep up with Acid House beats.

We approached the group and, after brief introductions, we asked if the warehouse belonged to them. Yes, was the reply, so we proposed a deal to hire it from them for one night. The guy doing all the talking was about six feet four inches tall, and had a big build and a bald head. He totally dismissed our suggestion and told us to forget the idea. We left feeling rather gutted that we hadn't found it before them, but this gripe quickly went out of our heads.

Keith called me a few days later to arrange a meeting. He sounded really anxious and wanted us to come over straight away. He'd negotiated a partnership deal on the grounds of finding a legal warehouse that held 5,000 people, and had already spoken to an owner who was waiting for Keith to get back to him. With stakes like this we had nothing to lose and bundles to gain.

Keith took us to the venue – the same one we'd seen days earlier in Clapton Pond! I couldn't believe it, and immediately counted a whole flock of chickens before they hatched. We asked the owner how much he was being paid to hire out the place and he told us £300. We immediately offered him £500 a night for five days: an offer he couldn't refuse. He was waiting for a deposit from the other firm and said that if he didn't have it by Wednesday the venue was ours.

That was the longest two days of my life, but we returned to the warehouse on the following Wednesday. The other mob had never showed and we didn't want to lose this venue, so we gave him two and a half grand there and then. He gave us the key, a hire lease (a handwritten bit of note paper) and our work began the next day.

I still couldn't believe those guys hadn't turned up; they must be crazy! I was very happy, though. Things were looking up: we had a legal warehouse that could hold 5,000 people and Christmas and New Year were just around the corner. This marked the beginning of a new era and the start of a roller-coaster ride through Heaven and Hell.

Our task of cleaning up had begun. Hundreds of used car tyres littered the building and we stacked them at one end of the warehouse before deciding to use them. A lot of thought went into the decor, which was very important to us. We wanted to create a party dreamland on a low budget. We brought a load more parachutes and some nets and got a real seven-foot Christmas tree. A bundle of new white canopies was nicked from a building site and we had inflatable props, fluorescent coloured card and ultraviolet coloured spray paint.

We used the tyres to build a large bar area and a semi-circle guard around the DJ console, then created a UV-lit tunnel at the entrance and covered it in canopies. The whole warehouse floor, including many oil puddles, was sprinkled with sawdust, which gave it a snow or cloud effect. The parachutes were fastened to the ceiling and the giant nets, sprayed with paint, were dangled from the roof in front of the DJ.

We fixed the projectors in various areas and built plastic cages around the inflatable props: one a skeleton, the other a multicoloured gorilla (the only ones we could get). Then we covered the Christmas tree with pieces of fluorescent card and stuck a UV over it; the reflections from the card looked better than the real lights. We'd created an ultimate party dreamland: now all that was needed were the bodies to fill it.

The printer did us 500 flyers and we spent the whole weekend promoting the Christmas Eve gig. Then one morning, just as we were back in the warehouse slogging our guts out to get it finished in time, we were having a spliff break when the entrance door was booted in. It was the big skinhead bloke we'd met on our first visit there. He had a sawn-off shotgun in his hand and was going berserk.

'You nicked my venue, you cunts,' he said.

'Hold on a minute, mate. You either use that shooter or listen to what we have to say,' I answered.

'No, *you* fucking listen: this place is mine, do you understand?' He walked up to me, pointing the gun at my head.

'Look, calm down. You were meant to pay the deposit last week but never showed. What did you expect us to do?' asked KP.

'Where's the owner?' the skinhead said, lowering the gun.

NUTT! I headbutted him square on the nose and grabbed the arm that held the shooter. KP took a run and whacked him over the head with a lump of wood. He fell to the floor, dropping the shooter in the process. KP quickly picked it up and shoved it in his face.

'Now you listen and you listen good. We don't want any trouble. It's your own fuckin' fault you lost the gaff, not ours. If you want to see anyone about it see the guvnor.'

He nodded, and we slowly let him up. 'You're right, I'm sorry, mate. It's just when I heard you were in here I thought you were taking the piss,' he said.

'OK,' I answered. 'Look, you better go and not come back unless you want a war.'

We searched him for more shells and found four in his pocket and two up the spout. We took them off him, gave him back the firearm and fucked him off. I wouldn't say I was a fighter I hate violence. I've always liked money, beautiful women and living a good life. Keith likes the same things as me but we're both as game as a beagle. In certain situations instinct takes over and you do what you have to if you want to survive. I had to sit down for a while after he went; my heart was beating faster than when I've been rushing.

The next day, on a wet afternoon, the entrance door to the warehouse swung open and in walked two guys and a gorgeous chick.

'Hi, my name's Tony Colston-Hayter,' one of the geezers said. 'I run Sunrise. Have you heard of me?'

'Yeah, we've heard of you. What about it?' I said.

'We're looking for a venue to stage a Christmas party. How about letting us join up with you guys? I had 4,000 at my last party in Greenwich.'

Then two more guys came walking in from the back of the warehouse, which made Keith lose his rag. 'What you fuckin' doing?'

'It's OK, they're with me,' said Tony.

Keith wanted to do them for sneaking about, but he calmed down after a few minutes and we got to talking.

This time we had a legal venue so we knew that even if we couldn't fill it at first, once word got out it would be rammed.

'We don't really need any help,' I said.

'I'll bring 4,000 people with me and we'll split the profit fifty-fifty. What do you say?'

Sunrise had already staged the biggest dance party in the country, so I knew he could deliver exactly what he claimed. I told him we wanted to do Christmas ourselves but would think about sharing a New Year's Eve. Tony was happy with this arrangement and exchanged numbers before leaving.

We knew loads of girls who'd agreed to hand out flyers for us, which was great. They were a good-looking bunch who created a buzz when they were together. They'd just shout 'Genesis, this Saturday!' at the top of their voices to attract maximum attention. Before you knew it, the flyers had all been given out and the girls just yelled the details out. It was hard work but we enjoyed it tremendously. We got a good reception at each club we flew around, making sure everyone leaving got a flyer.

Driving around London during the early hours of the morning is really tiring. Then you'd be up at the crack of dawn running about doing the stuff that could only be done in office hours. This usually amounted to more promoting, putting yourself about, making sure everyone knew where and when. There was always something to do, even if it meant doing odd jobs in the warehouse. Late lie-ins simply didn't fit our schedule. We'd be out continually, reminding people about the gig and maximising the hype.

Genesis, Genesis, Genesis: we ate, spoke and lived only Genesis. This was something we deeply believed in, it wasn't just about having parties. We were all bearing witness to a happily unified nation and projecting good karma to one another, which was well worth the graft. Under that roof we forgot our troubles and those of the mad world around us. We were fully interacting with people whom under normal circumstances we'd have passed by in the street without a glance. We knew it was something special.

GETTING SORTED

The meeting point for our Christmas Eve gig was the Lea Valley ice rink on Lea Bridge Road. We sent somebody to man the point at 10 p.m., and within fifteen minutes about 100 cars pulled up outside the warehouse. We had an instant queue of 300 people who were all really excited about finding the party. My sister Teena was taking the money at the door and I stood at the end of the tunnel so that I could see the look on their faces as they walked into our man-made vortex.

When the first guests came through the hanging canopies their facial expressions were full of amazement. They could see time and great effort had gone into making this night memorable and successful. We were given the rubber stamp of approval by each guest who came through the door, which pleased us no end. I felt like the man from Del Monte had said yes.

Although we didn't know it at the time, this event put us up into the premier league of organisers and promoters. We'd only actually booked four doormen that night, a few guys Keith knew, and we got swamped with people. By midnight, 600 pilled-up fanatics were holding hands and chanting 'Aceeed, Aceeed, Aceeed!' We felt real proud – our dream was a success and it was all down to us.

The decor worked wonders at enhancing the effect of the Ecstasy, and together they generated a euphoric atmosphere. I remember loads of different people telling me how fantastic the Christmas tree lights were. What lights? It was just small pieces of fluorescent cardboard under a UV!

Even the police were great. They drove past a few times, asking our doorman if everything was OK. A rumour circulated that undercover cops were poking around inside. But, at the end of the day, I was a user, not a dealer. I had nothing to hide. I was very strict about bods blatantly taking drugs or skinning up in plain view of everyone.

People got a real shock when I instructed them not to be so open about the drugs. 'Who are you?' they'd ask, and I'd tell them it was my party. They'd say, 'This is an Acid party, are you joking, or what?' I assured them I wasn't joking and they did as I asked, not believing what they'd just heard. But this was possibly the only legal site in the whole of England and we weren't going to lose it for anybody. It wasn't just that we were trying to keep the drug abuse covert and all the good qualities overt. It only needed one journalist to snap someone off their nut and the Old Bill would be all over us like a rash. While I was making my way to the decks I came across a young boy who looked about fifteen. He'd got his head back and was looking at the ceiling with arms outstretched by his sides, turning around in circles. The flyer clearly stated that our party, warehouse or not, was strictly for over-eighteens only. I'd no idea how he'd got past my sister. I said he had to leave and take whoever came with him, which turned out to be his brother and his pals.

'You'd better take me to your brother,' I said.

We went up to a group of about seven guys. I told his brother I thought the kid was too young to be there and he punched me in the face. Before it all went completely wobbly, I told him who I was. A load of my pals suddenly appeared behind me, asking if everything was all right. I turned to the brother and said that he'd better leave right now, and that if I were a different person I'd serve him up. But, as it was Christmas, I escorted them to the door, gave their money back and told them to piss off.

The attendance for that night was about 900 and a brilliant time was had by all. At 10 a.m. on Christmas Day, 200 people sang 'We Wish you a Merry Christmas' and Christmas carols. I hadn't seen crowds harmonising like that since going to football many years before. Everybody introduced themselves to each other and wished Merry Christmas to all. By noon everyone had gone home except for a few friends who stayed behind. I was having a piss in a corner when I found a bag of class-A substances. There was some powder, Es and Thai grass. I sat down with the others and shared out its contents.

I didn't want the Es because I had to eat dinner later that day. If I couldn't eat my Christmas dinner my mum would kill me. But I chopped up some long lines of charlie (hoping that the buzz would wear off in time for dinner) and we had a good old sniff.

There were ten of us left in the warehouse, all good friends, so I decided to put a few more tunes on and we danced until 2 p.m. My two partners and I hugged and congratulated each other and gave one another a grand as a present. We went back to our parents' houses for dinner. My mum always lays on a delicious spread and works hard to make the day perfect. I didn't eat much and soon passed out on the sofa. My mum and stepfather had bought my sisters a karaoke machine each, so the house was going off severely. I only managed to sing one track all the way through: 'You've Lost that Lovin' Feeling' by the Righteous Brothers.

We returned to the warehouse that night to start cleaning up in preparation for Chapter Three in a few days' time. We could have paid somebody else to do it, but in those days for some reason promoters did everything themselves: from flyposting to cleaning.

We were pinning some decorations to the warehouse ceiling when two policemen walked in. They asked if we were the organisers because they wanted to see some kind of document stating the building's exact terms of use. Whenever we were in the building I would make sure I had the lease with me, and gave it to the officers. It said the owner was leasing the building to us for private music-business parties. Dibble wrote the details in their notebooks and left.

We were lost for words, and stared at each other with huge grins. The police were giving us full permission to continue arranging dance parties. Don't forget that these were times when party organisers would run a mile at the mere sight of the Old Bill. I was facing them head on by producing documentation of the fact that this event had the full blessing of the owner. There was nothing they could do, not that they wanted to stop it in the first place: they couldn't give a shite what we were doing so long as it wasn't dodgy.

Most of the Old Bill hadn't even heard of Ecstasy at this point. To older folk, we were a bunch of kids who were having parties in warehouses and not even drinking alcohol. The pubs and clubs gave them more trouble than we did. Once police had established that it was a legal, safe building and no alcohol was being sold, they'd give you the OK. Obviously it helped if you conducted yourself in a professional manner, maybe even claiming that you represented a major entertainment company. The authorities' main concern back then was the safety and fire regulations. Once they were checked and passed, you avoided the hassle of being harassed by the police and fire department. If you were sensible you'd make sure the venue was safe, clean and not derelict, which would enforce the general belief that they were legal venues.

Our venue was now almost ready for our next party, and we were running around like lunatics. Genesis was becoming the talk of London. Now we could print 500 flyers with the actual venue address rather than a meeting point. Most people knew where it was by this time anyway, and now that the Old Bill had seen our brief we could be as bold as brass.

The Christmas period had been chaotic, to say the least, and now we were about to organise our third party in a matter of days on Boxing Day. We'd slogged our guts out through the festive season and so far it had been worth every minute. The door receipts were better than expected and we had become a clubland name.

We'd never thought about how many people would turn up. We wanted to stage the best gig, but having the biggest parties didn't enter our heads. To have 900 people show was more than we could ever have asked for. As far as we were concerned, things could only get better.

In the blink of an eye, Boxing Day was upon us and it was time to get busy. At 9 p.m. a large queue was forming outside, and we weren't even open for another hour. Our lighting man was having trouble with the electric mains through some technical problem I didn't understand. About 300 people were lined up outside in the cold winter air and although we hadn't fixed our electrical problem we decided to let them in. The first 100 were let in free as a gesture of goodwill. Candles flickered around the warehouse as the technicians went through their fault-finding process.

It took an hour before lights and sound system were restored, which was met by a roar of applause. The first track on the decks was 'Can You Feel It?' by Fingers

Inc., which got everyone straight in the mood and hands went immediately into the air. Before we knew it, 2,000 thrill-seekers were absolutely going for it. We were caught completely by surprise as again we only had four doormen.

The drinks stocks wouldn't last for long, so four different vans were sent out to find more supplies. Luckily, the vans came back half-filled and we didn't run out of drinks the whole night. The drivers told how they had walked into 7–11 and bought every drink in the building. We didn't get any discount and paid retail price, leaving all the other customers with nothing to drink!

The party was peaking and the DJ was playing an electric set. I got introduced to quite a few celebrities that night, including Matt Dillon, Milli Vanilli, Boy George and Derek B. I also met some of the West End's biggest club owners, who in their own words had 'come to see what all the fuss was about.' They'd come to see where their punters had disappeared to and were gutted to find they'd lost them to a party in an old warehouse on a backstreet in east London. Yet we weren't intentionally stepping on any toes because we were miles from any of the clubs in the area. In any case, this was a different concept to all the other clubs, which were basically still discos.

One of the perks of being a promoter was the fact we were on every club and concert guest list in the country. We could bring as many people with us as we wanted, and get a free bottle of champagne thrown in. You'd walk into a club and get five different wraps of charlie put in your hand by dealers who wanted to be on our guest list. You'd have a trail of women from the door to the bar and then no one would let you buy a single drink.

These were hangers-on: women would let us use and abuse them just to be in the company of well-known party promoters. It was a two-way thing: we'd let them hang out with us if they let us live out some schoolboy fantasy. The girls would keep us entertained for days after the parties; we used to grab a few from our party and take them home with us. While other people went to early-morning post-party parties at clubs and bars, we had our own private drug-and-sex orgy: a couple of mates and a motor full of beautiful chicks.

Tony from Sunrise came to see us that day and asked if we'd made our mind up about co-promoting the New Year's Eve party five days later. Even though we could get 2,000 people on our own, the warehouse was still only partially filled. I knew joining with Sunrise would be a positive move and beneficial to us all. We were the biggest promoters in the east of London, and they were the biggest in the west. If we worked together it was possible to capture the whole market and produce the best and biggest events in England.

Our decision was yes, so we immediately began planning the night ahead. We made up some photocopied flyers because there wasn't time for printers to make any original ones. This time, our aim was to stage the biggest Acid House party the world had ever seen.

GENESIS SUNSET CHAPTER THREE: THE FUTURE IS NOW

At 8 p.m. on a cold New Year's Eve we were standing outside the warehouse in deep discussion with a police chief about the event scheduled for later that night. Tony Colston-Hayter and myself were trying to convince the officer this was a genuine music-business showcase for invited guests only.

The inspector insisted on looking around the large warehouse for fire risks or anything else that could be viewed as dangerous. The interior of the warehouse had already been transformed into a full-scale twilight zone. Giant stage props were strategically placed around the venue and we'd hired lighting and sound companies to supply the equipment and co-design the finished effects. The venue and operation team looked very professionally coordinated and the security wore penguin suits and communicated via radio.

Some local Del Boy had sold us a van filled with fire extinguishers, illuminated EXIT signs and crash barriers. We made sure fire regulations were implemented and anything flammable was removed or sprayed with fire-resistant chemicals. Little did the chief know we'd only started decorating earlier that day. Although the interior couldn't be faulted, he still wasn't happy about letting the event take place.

We insisted on our legal rights to be on the property with the landlord's full blessing and showed our documentation. In fact we were quite within our rights to ask him to leave the building and only return with a court order or warrant. We told Dibble we had 1,000 especially invited guests from the world's music industry, ranging from celebrities to major record company MDs. Stepping on our toes could lead to massive law suits and huge compensation fines.

The discussion between ourselves and the officer was conducted in a courteous manner. We knew our legal rights and had full confidence in our presentation. An icy wind ripped through our cotton suits and my hands were frozen to the clipboard I held tight to my body. Our blag involved moody celebrity guest lists, band schedules and other false info. Our adrenaline was flowing.

After 45 minutes of us giving out the biggest load of bullshit you've ever heard, the chief decided to bring in a fire inspector to make the final decision. The station was ten minutes away so we hoped the inspector would hurry to get here: in less than two hours this street and the surrounding area would be invaded by outsiders.

I walked back into the warehouse, giving Tony a sly signal to keep the copper just where he was. Shit! I had thunderbolts ripping through my stomach! I'd just remembered that after our Christmas Eve party, due to our rush to get home for Christmas dinner, we'd swept and left thousands of plastic bottles, cans and general rubbish on the fire escape at the back of the warehouse.

I broke out into an instant sweat. All our hard work could be on the verge of being fucked. I called out to the security team and told them a fire chief was on his way and the cans had to be cleared from the fire escapes. They sprang into immediate action, grabbing anything that could scoop the rubbish up. We slammed out through one of the fire doors and nearly passed out.

A mass of cans and bottles lay before us, knee-deep. We started throwing the cans into bags and over the wall. We formed a line and frantically cleaned the surrounding area of any obstacles. Each of us got dirty and sticky from all the shit that poured out of the rubbish. Amazingly, in only 30 minutes we'd almost finished.

I decided to see what was happening out front. Tony was still engrossed in conversation with the officer on the merits of what we were doing. However, the chief didn't want the responsibility of a thousand party revellers congregating on his manor. It was stalemate.

We were expecting a huge turn-out that night so we'd hired a professional security team. A good friend of mine named Ed, who had been a marine for most of his life, had told me he knew some mean, highly trained motherfuckers who had gone AWOL from the army. They had been in the special services for more than ten years before deciding to establish an international agency of their own. The geezers lived on the outskirts of London and spent most of their time abroad. They all had their own special skills, learnt in the paratroopers, navy or whatever infantry divisions they had signed up to. The men were very disciplined, worked really well together and were gentle but firm.

We paid them £1,500 for a team of fifteen, with a further ten members as back-up if required. This was a lot more money than we would have paid a pub or club doorman, who usually earned between £30 and £50 a night. But these guys were worth every penny. They'd been shot at, fought behind enemy lines, and had come back telling jokes about the things they'd done.

Tony brought his own team of six who were also from out of London and they treated the event like a military operation. The governor justified the high fee by telling us his men would stand firm against anything, even if a shooter was stuck in their mush. No one would be leaving the building with any money belonging to us.

Being robbed was our main concern because, in a lot of interested people's eyes, we were making dodgy money. We weren't regarded as an entertainment company staging extravagant special events. To blaggers, robbing us could be easier than doing a bank and there could even be more dosh involved. It was very important for us to have the right team around us: geezers who wouldn't bottle it if they were faced with armed robbers.

Anyway, I looked back down the dark street and spotted a tall thin man walking along the road with his head down. The policeman happily announced the arrival of the fire chief and walked towards him, closely followed by us.

'They're planning some kind of party,' the Old Bill said. 'We don't want it and I'm sure it's not safe. Have a look. It's down to you.'

The fireman didn't look very happy at the fact that he'd had to break away from the festivities back at the station. I looked at him and thought we had no chance. He was in his late forties, grey hair, stone-cold Cockney accent, and looked bloody efficient. He'd given Dibble a boost to say the least.

By this time my thoughts were going ballistic. Why us? Why now? I wondered if the fire guy was prepared to take a bribe, as I told him all about the strict fire regulations at our events. Our illuminated EXIT signs were clearly visible, as was our variety of stolen fire-extinguishers. So we all entered the warehouse, where our lighting technicians were running through their routines.

You can't even imagine how I felt as I watched these two middle-aged blokes, who had no understanding of our culture and the kind of event we were trying to stage, deciding whether our party could go on. I could hardly believe my ears when the fire chief turned to the Old Bill and said, 'Everything seems fine to me. As far as I'm concerned they can have their party.'

We felt like crying! Our whole mind, body and soul was in this event and the police and fire department had given us a green light to print money and change the future! I would quite happily have given them five grand each. All they would have had to do was drop me the slightest of hints and it would have been theirs.

On this particular night, we had decided to open another part of the warehouse which was a third of the size of the main room, and connected to it by a short tunnel. We put three inflatable bouncy castles and some fan lights into the chamber, then added another sound system with double decks.

The large room itself had our command centre in the corner. Lined up on a long table were all the phones, about ten in all, which would ring constantly until 6 a.m. People would be calling from all over the country to find out exactly where the venue was located and if the party was still on. This was part of the excitement: finding your way to a warehouse party was almost as good as actually being there.

At 10 p.m. a 500-strong gathering of the happiest, most excited thrill-seekers you could ever lay your eyes on cheered and clapped as we officially announced the gig open. On the stroke of midnight a thousand E'd-up party animals held their hands in the air and sang Joe Smooth's anthem 'Promised Land'. Picture this: a huge art deco warehouse; thousands of ecstatic people, most of whom were experiencing their first Ecstasy tabs (Calies) and parties. We danced and sang at the top of our voices: 'Brothers, sisters, one day we will be free, from trouble and violence, people fighting in the street.' We sang the song word for word. Wow, what a russssshh. I wanted it to last for ever! We'd booked some really talented DJs, including Terry Farley, Tony Wilson, Eddie Richards, Fat Tony, Phil and Ben, and Colin Hudd. The building was old and had seen better days and this made it a security coordinator's worst nightmare. The floor we intended to use was in good shape, but there were three other floors, all with broken doors and windows.

The ground floor windows were covered with heavy-duty backdrops, and the main staircase from the first level down was blocked off with hundreds of used car tyres. There was no lighting on the fire escape out back or above ground level and the restricted areas were cornered off and in total darkness.

We were in our command centre counting the loot when a call on the walkie-talkie informed us the building was under siege by hundreds of people hellbent on bunking in! They were trying to gain entrance by any means necessary, including violence. Our security was stretched to the max and struggled to regain control of the fire escape, where a group of geezers were throwing bricks and rubble at them. It was pitch-black out there. We brought our guys inside to man the exit doors and sent out a call for reinforcements. Our home-made tyre barricade on the first floor was trashed, and twenty-odd geezers were taunting the doorman from the upper level. Some people on the fire escape made unsuccessful attempts to cut through our backdrops with knives and broken glass. An arsenal of weapons was brought into the office to protect us and the cash.

It didn't take long for the back-up team to arrive, and control was quickly restored and the building fully secured, without any casualties. Then my mates from down the pub in Hackney turned up in fancy-dress costumes, shouting 'Aceeed!' I couldn't believe it: Crimble, Blond, Short, Scarfee, Lloyd, Scrap Iron and Buff running around introducing themselves to everyone! *Here* was first-hand evidence that Ecstasy enhanced happy feelings towards others! These guys were ex-blaggers who loved a punch-up and only weeks ago told me they'd attack anyone who hugged them, and here they were hugging anyone who walked by. Not only that: they were dancing! These geezers had never danced anywhere before! But this was a dramatic transformation I was happy to witness.

The same change was taking place simultaneously across London and the Home Counties and up north. Before long, the whole country was projecting love and harmony on the dance floor, at home and at work. There was so much energy in the warehouse that I think, if you really concentrated and had meditation experience, you could levitate purely on the vibe. I know it sounds like bollocks and one of those mad thoughts you get while you're buzzing, but I have to admit that I did try it!

Sadly our party had to end at 10 a.m., although there were still hundreds of enthusiastic punters desperately clinging on to the vibe. We thanked them all for turning up, then kicked them out. The money had already been divided between me and Tony and secured in separate safe houses nearby. The security team wasn't really needed so we sent them home, which left six people in the building. Keith, Tony, KP and I were in the back office counting what was left of the pound coins taken at the bar. There must have been three grand in ten-pound stacks on the table. We heard the sound of voices in the corridor outside and Keith and KP went to investigate, thinking it could be the Old Bill.

I heard them saying the area was out of bounds, but an agitated voice said they were looking for the promoters. I grabbed an iron bar from the table and told Tony to get security on the mobile. The office door crashed open and a tall skinny geezer came charging into the tiny narrow room. I whacked him hard and he fell to the ground. Tony was wrestling with a second intruder and I whacked him in the nut as well for good measure.

In the corridor my partners were fighting with three more geezers. We retreated into the office and searched for more weapons. Armed with two knives, a knuckle-duster and an iron bar, we stepped back into the arena. The group was heading our way, with knives, bricks and lumps of wood. Like wildcats trapped in a corner, we ran towards the attackers, but Linford Christie would have had trouble catching up with them. We couldn't.

The security showed up shortly afterwards. We told them what had occurred and off they went. The team returned empty-handed, which I was glad about really because the intruders had already accepted defeat. If our doormen had got hold of them it could well have got very messy!

The partnership between Genesis and Sunrise was a major success and we'd achieved our objective of staging the biggest and best Acid party in the world. Even *NME* voted our New Year's Eve event Best Party of 1988. We had three black bags of dosh, which we split fifty-fifty and everybody – Tony and us – was happy.

We decided to promote a series of events together, with the next one on the following Saturday. However, the bubble burst on the Wednesday when the local police chief paid us a personal visit at the warehouse. He told us the building didn't belong to the person who had leased it to us. Even worse, the geezer was a squatter and had no rights at all. The chief wasn't arrogant about it but simply said we couldn't have any more events there and we had to clear our stuff out by the following week. He even apologised for bringing the bad news. We were shocked but knew there was no chance of continuing at that venue. It was time to hit the road.

GENESIS SUNSET: AGAINST ALL ODDS

Unfortunately, nobody wanted to rent warehouses to promoters, which meant venues were hard to come by.

The clubs didn't have the facilities to accommodate our huge crowds, and the few that were big enough to hold thousands of people closed too early. This left an enormous gap, which had to be filled. We knew that if we didn't grab the opportunity to stage even better parties than before, somebody else would do it.

The difference between us and a lot of rival promoters was that we chose safe buildings with a minimal risk of harm for our punters. Some promoters didn't share our concern, and staged events in derelict warehouses. Once we'd found a site we'd forge lease documents to pretend to cover ourselves legally. One of our workers would spend a day collecting property-for-sale lists and other literature that featured an estate agent's logo. We never targeted any particular company; we picked the agents at random. Then the typed text was covered with a perfectly cut, blank sheet of paper, leaving the header and bottom exposed. We'd stick the paper down with glue and photocopy it ten times, to allow for any mistakes.

The blank letter-headed paper was then taken to an old friend of the family, Leigh, who was the only staunch person we knew with a typewriter. It couldn't be taken to just anyone: we didn't want to divulge our methods for others to copy. Leigh would knock up a script to my specification. It wasn't an elaborate blag and got straight to the point. The end product was an apparently legally binding document that proved we had hired the building through the correct channels and stated the exact intended use of the premises for all to see. The lease would read as follows:

This document is to confirm the use of (Venue Address) as a location for private music-business functions. The project manager is (Name) who represents the (EMI, or Sony, or Virgin) recording company.

For further details please contact this department during office hours only, or consult the project manager for a full brief of events.

Yours sincerely,   *Yours sincerely,*

Special Projects Department   *Manager*
(EMI, Sony, Virgin)   *(Estate Agent)*

Then we'd photocopy the original typed document and keep one on the site of any building we crashed. We claimed The Public Entertainment Act 1982 kept us within the law.

If someone found a suitable building, we'd offer them a deal. Some promoters called Pasha located a big warehouse in east London, which we agreed to use. We decided to start a membership club and made the announcement on the flyer. We wanted to project a good vibe when printing our flyers, so we printed a short story on a birthday-card-styled flyer. On one side was the hype and on the other was the event information. We decided to call our promotion company 'Young Minds Entertainment'. The hype read as follows:

The Genesis chapters began in a small deserted London street, where three young minds pulled together in the hope of bringing a new light to the world of entertainment, calling this form of entertainment Genesis.

For the support and encouragement from you, the people who make everything possible, we are truly thankful. We offer to you our very own exclusive limited Members Club and promise the struggle will continue!

Summer of Love
Winter of Joy
Year of Genesis

We went to view the warehouse and found it was OK to use. The building was U-shaped. The River Thames flowed past a big yard where there was a docking bay for small boats, and mounted on the wall was a royal crest. The section we planned to use had already been broken into so all we had to do was bring our team in to set everything up.

It was 5 p.m. and dark as our vans drove towards the site entrance. A geezer appeared and opened the gates. We had four trucks of equipment and a big van full of soft drinks. After the last truck drove through the iron gates, they were closed and padlocked. Whoever was on site would have the moody estate agent document, which stated the usual bullshit. Although I'd made up the documents I would never sign them myself so that, if I got arrested and my handwriting sampled, it wouldn't come back to me.

Only one part of the building was going to be used, but it could hold 4,000 people. Our crew and the lighting and sound guys had now mastered the art of transforming a venue in a matter of hours, and this was coordinated on site by myself, KP or Keith. We found a secure office upstairs on a balcony that overlooked the factory floor, which by now resembled a high-tech dance arena. The office had no windows and only one entrance.

The electrics were turned on by a cab driver I'd met while I was giving out flyers one night. His name was WD and he spoke with a slight American accent. I was outside the Wag Club when I was introduced to a chap named Jerry who used to control all the minicabs. Jerry asked me if we needed a cab rank outside our venue, which was a great idea because most parties were held on industrial estates; the nearest cab office was usually at least three miles away – if you were lucky! You'd always end up with thousands of people walking the streets in the early hours of Sunday morning still buzzing from the party. Anyway, Jerry introduced me to WD, who turned out to be a wizard electrician. He gave me all his telephone numbers and said we could call him at any time, day or night. He came to the warehouse, took one look at the fuse box, and within half an hour we had full electricity. Power!

Before we knew it, 9 p.m. was upon us. The meeting point was outside a warehouse in Leaside Road. We left someone there to tell everyone the party address; our names were so big at this point that we didn't even need to promote the event. We had a 3,000-strong following ready to go anywhere we told them.

At all times the man at the meeting point had to keep control of the traffic flow. We had to maintain a high level of professionalism at all levels. If Dibble saw anything getting out of control, they could move us on and block roads leading to the venue, which would make life very difficult. So we deployed more staff to stop cars and give them the venue details. We made small foldable signs that read GENESIS SUNSET MEETING POINT and when cars stopped we'd give them a map and move them on. There were at least ten people doing this around a two-mile radius of the warehouse. A few thousand pocket-sized maps were printed, showing the venue and surrounding

GENESIS SUNSET: AGAINST ALL ODDS

area. The map had the Genesis logo in the corner and the full address handwritten on the back, which was a job in itself. My mum and sisters wrote each of them and it took them about five hours.

The man at the point wouldn't release any of the maps until he got the word from us. Because this was an illegal event, we had to be sure we could scare up an instant crowd. We figured if we had a thousand people inside the building and we fronted the Old Bill as the organisers, there was a good chance the event would go ahead, because the last thing Dibble wanted was thousands of people driving around the streets.

We made the call and instructed the guy at the meeting point to give out the maps. I asked how many people were there and was told the roads were completely blocked already. The building was secured and a single doorway was used as an entrance and exit. We put a table by the door and prepared to be bombarded by revellers. There were security with dogs on the main gate, to stop anyone driving into the yard. Within fifteen minutes, cars began parking in the streets surrounding the venue. A queue was building up inside the yard of around 800 people. I was summoned to the gate because a chief of police, together with 40 other officers, was standing in front of the gates and stopping everyone from coming in.

Because of my previous encounters with law enforcement, I half-knew what I could get away with and some of the private property laws. I also knew there was no way Dibble could find out whether we had permission to be there, at this time of night. Armed with this knowledge, I went out to the gate with the confidence of a pop star. Thrusting the moody leasing document into the chief's hands, I ordered the officers to take a few steps back off this privately owned land. They complied, and I tuned my focus on to the chief.

'My name is Claude Ferdinand,' I said. 'I represent Virgin Records and this is a private launch party to celebrate a forthcoming album by one of our artists.'

The chief closely inspected the lease agreement before asking me why the local police station wasn't informed of the event. I told him that wasn't my department and he should take it up with my superiors.

Right at that moment, fire bells rang out from inside the building. I asked the officer if he would remain there whilst I attended to the alarm. He nodded, and I ran off and around the corner where 12 security men were waiting for me. I told them to smash the bells off the walls and we started with the two in the yard. We were hitting the bells with scaffold poles, hammers and huge steel cutters. As we knocked each one down we'd hear another going off somewhere else. Each one we knocked off was met with a roar of applause and cheers from the queue of people in the yard. To make matters worse, we had to break into other parts of the building that we weren't even going to use.

In half an hour we'd gone through around 30 doors and knocked down about 25 red bells. We were out of breath, but had achieved our main objective, which was to stop the bells ringing. Knocking them off was the only way they could be stopped. Otherwise, the police would close the party down, private property or not. It wasn't as if we exactly had a key to the alarm.

Calming myself down, I went back around to the police chief, who was impatiently awaiting my return. I apologised to the officer and explained the delay by saying that I held a large set of keys to the whole building and had been struggling to discover which one operated the system.

I went on to inform him that this was a private event and everyone who entered the premises had to have a valid invite. The police had the road and gate blocked, so people were jumping over a perimeter wall. The chief asked me why they were hopping over the wall, and I said it was because we had an international line-up of artists contracted to appear and the event was not only unique but an historic celebration of the music world.

'So what do you plan on doing with the people jumping over the wall?' asked Dibble.

'I have 45 highly trained security members on site who can deal with any situation that may arise,' I replied.

The chief looked impressed and told me that if I had any problems with gatecrashers I should dial 999 and the police would help me to handle it. I asked him to write his name and a direct telephone number that I could contact his station on. The chief of police took my pen and the clipboard and wrote his details on the moody lease! I couldn't believe it! My show of confidence had paid off! The blag had worked because he didn't want to take the chance of being wrong. He'd even signed our fake document! What a result!

When I walked back into the yard the whole team was waiting for me. We were all screaming and going mad: we'd done it, and the party was on! The fun had already started inside and, when I announced over the PA system that the police had gone, a loud cheer ripped through the building and the energy level gained another notch. Two hours later, 4,000 people were crammed inside and there were another 700 out in the yard. People were dancing everywhere and on top of anything they could find.

I was spending a lot of time in our makeshift office with Tony and two other members of staff. We were the quickest at counting money and there was a constant flow of uncounted cash in carrier bags for us to count and log on to our balance sheets. We had two of the hardest security team members outside the door and nearby were two other guys from the unit with shooters, who were standing ten yards from the door and watching it like hawks.

The security team were there to prevent any attempted armed robbery. They would die before anyone took any money, and they looked as mean as fuck. Even though they knew we were paying their money they wouldn't say a thing to us, not even 'Hello'. These guys were scary motherfuckers who looked like a tribe of Arnie's Terminators.

I was glad they were on my side: I'd hate one of them to come bursting through my front door. The scariest thing about those geezers was that they were very organised and disciplined. They were capable of kidnapping you from under the nose of the woman you were in bed with and she wouldn't know a thing until the next morning. In a nutshell, they were lean, mean, fighting machines with no regard for human life. Yet the fact of the matter was that we needed a team like this so no one could mess with our money or welfare. They weren't bullies or horrible to our punters; they were perfect gentlemen and showed respect to everyone who entered the building. Everybody was searched for weapons, then welcomed to the pleasure dome.

We were in the office carrying out the usual duties: counting money, paying wages and snorting charlie. Then one of the workers knocked repeatedly on the door and when we let him in he went straight into a panic. Sweat was pouring down his red face and he was breathless from running. I tried to calm him down.

'Wayne, I don't want to panic you, but somebody has just collapsed and died downstairs,' he said.

WHAT?! A cold shiver crept up my spine and goose pimples immediately covered my body. I stood there in complete shock and asked him if he was sure of what he had just said. He assured me he was 100% positive and that he had tried to revive the bloke himself but had got no response.

The hairs on my head and the back of my neck stood on end, my heart pounded and sweat soaked my shirt. I told the guy to take me to the body and told Keith to take the money to the safe house, just in case. So far we had collected about 50 grand and most of it was at the safe house already.

We walked around the balcony that looked over the dance floor and I looked down at the thousands of happy faces. I felt saddened that someone had died at one of our events, then suddenly snapped out of it at the thought of being arrested for murder or something along those lines.

Once the Old Bill found out we'd broken and entered the building to stage an illegal dance party where someone had died, a judge would beyond all doubt hand out a stiff prison sentence to the organisers and make an example of us to would-be promoters and drug dealers. I became angry that this person who I'd never even heard of was about to bring our world to an abrupt end. No matter what anyone said, we didn't ask him to take drugs and he did not take drugs in our company.

We were making our way through the crowds, our minds in turmoil. Shit, shit, shit, why us, and why now? My brain slipped into survival mode. If the police were brought in we'd definitely get locked up on some big charges. I was left with two choices: call Old Bill or arrange for someone to take the body to a hospital, claiming they found it lying in the street. I'd be prepared to give a few grand to the person who took the body there. It may sound callous, but I wasn't going to prison for anyone.

We approached a group of people who were standing around. A guy was slumped motionless on the floor. I pushed through the circle that had gathered around him to see what was happening. Kneeling down, I checked his vital signs: there was a slight pulse! I slapped him hard around the face a few times, shaking him, and seconds later he was coughing and breathing.

He opened his eyes and everybody cheered. A feeling of relief came over me. I gave him a drink of water, and helped him to stand up. You could tell he'd taken an E because his jaw started shaking wildly. His friends were all hugging and kissing us both, but when they calmed down I asked the guy who he was with and he pointed to about ten people. I asked them to follow me to the entrance door, where I gave them their money back and told them not to come back, ever.

This may seem harsh but this whole scenario had caused me enormous grief and made me think in certain ways I had no desire to revisit. If it wasn't enough having to worry about Dibble and armed robbers, now we had to worry about people dying because of Ecstasy.

My girlfriend was a vocalist for an indie band and didn't really like the music we played at my gigs. However, when I returned home after the east London party she told me she'd never realised how big my events actually were. While she was parked in her car at some traffic lights in Oxford Street, a coach crammed with people pulled alongside her and asked whether she knew where the Genesis party was located. Imagine that: out of all the people these partygoers could have stopped for directions, they choose my girlfriend! Truly, Acid House was taking over the world.

GENESIS SUNSET: HEDONISM

Hedonism was set to be our seventh event in a matter of weeks and Genesis was now infamous throughout the country. No other promoters would even think about staging an event on the same night as we did. Most people who came to our events had never experienced anything quite like this before. Once they entered this world they became instantly hooked. There was nowhere on the planet that could compare to what was taking place in London.

A lost generation had found its direction and secured a place in cult history. Punks, mods, rockers, hippies, skinheads, rude boys, Hell's Angels, soul boys, teds, casuals and now, in 1989, the Acid House phenomenon. Popping pills has been a part of most cults since day one: back in the Sixties people dropped uppers and downers like there was a world shortage. Blues, Dexys, Valium, Black Bombers and Mogadons were just a few examples of the tablets that were taken back then. However, these pills didn't draw anyone together or break down any barriers between different cultures.

Then the LSD factor came into play and the Western world went psychedelic. The hippies were very much in line with our Acid House dream except that they didn't unite all races under one roof. It was too soon after the oppression of the Fifties and the masses just weren't ready for it. The hippie movement was a peaceful fun-loving cult who loved and respected all life and their fellow man. I can 100% relate to this, except we didn't have the option of free love like they did back then. The Aids factor came into play in the Eighties and left the next generation with no alternative but to seek pleasure and enjoyment elsewhere.

Yet Ecstasy united black, white, yellow and brown people as one. At any big dance party there was an across-the-board mixture of races holding hands and giving out total love and respect for one another. Ecstasy is an upper and was completely different to any other drug. The hysteria whipped up by people going to dance parties caused a massive surge of positive energy. The E generation became the We generation. We were making history, boldly going where no man had gone before.

1988 was a new dawn. Gone were the days when our parents could confidently claim that nothing could ever beat the Sixties. We still salute the artists from that era, The Beatles, The Stones, Hendrix and T Rex, but for us the men of power were Todd Terry, Larry Heard, Frankie Knuckles, Derrick May, Lil Louis Vega, Steve Hurley, Jamie Principle, Robert Owens, Jesse Saunders and Marshall Jefferson.

The hardest aspect of staging a huge event was finding the right venue. Sometimes we'd 'gain entrance' to four or five buildings before making our decision. Our hunting grounds were mainly industrial estates in east and north London. Our enthusiasm could sometimes lead to us being careless, which could easily have had dire consequences. There were times when we found ourselves hiding out in warehouses while police squads searched the area for us. It only needed one person to spot us jumping over the fence and call the Old Bill and we could be in serious trouble. The very last thing we wanted to do was get nicked for breaking into an empty warehouse.

The partnership between us and Tony was working out, so instead of heading our separate ways we decided to throw a series of extravaganzas in various warehouses around London. If we could have found a suitable legal location we'd have offered the landlords a mint and Keith's bird too(!), but finding such a gaff was nigh on impossible. Landlords were scared shitless by politicians and the threat of imprisonment, or at the very least a hefty fine.

Virtually every day we'd hit the road in search of warehouses, driving through industrial estates by day and promoting our events by night. We located a venue just off the A406 that was on two floors, and after a quick butcher's through the window we decided to crash it. Arranging the meeting point for this party would be easy because the North Circular is a major route to the M25, which meant most people wouldn't have to drive through town; people driving in convoy through the city would attract police interest.

As a rule, we never broke into the building before the night of the gig because a peek through the window is a good enough inspection and will provide you with the information needed to know if the gaff is suitable. Derelict warehouses were avoided for safety reasons as the police would never let the party go ahead if the gaff had loads of broken windows or rubble piled up outside.

The ideal solution was a disused building available for leasing. It didn't even matter if the electricity wasn't working: our sparky was a magician. Sometimes he'd even wire our sound and lighting systems to a street lamp, which had the capability to run every piece of equipment we needed.

We'd be giving out flyers outside clubs almost every night: the sheer buzz of our achievements kept the harsh, Antarctic conditions at bay. Enter the Dragon, Future, Camden Palace and Loud Noise were on our flyer distribution list. On three nights a week Heaven and the Soundshaft presented special club nights that were the focal point of the whole dance-party movement and were the longest running successful club nights in the whole of England. Once word got out from this circle that a particular party was in the brew, everybody waited in a state of excitement for the night of the gig.

Our next selected warehouse was on an industrial estate and surrounded by other storage warehouses. We wouldn't use a factory building, because most of them had old industrial machinery bolted to the floor. Around 5 p.m. on the evening of the event, under the cover of winter darkness, we slowly drove on to the estate. We knew exactly where all the night-watchman offices were because we'd cased the area during the week. Our pre-planned route took us around a labyrinth of buildings to avoid being seen, until we reached the loading-dock entrance to our chosen venue. We jumped out of the motor, armed with steel bolt cutters, and clasped the padlock that was holding the metal doors together. One movement of the arm rendered the lock useless and we drove the car inside.

We shone three torch beams to light up the huge interior. Keith started to look for the fuse box while we ran to the other end of the long building. There were around 100 cardboard boxes, approximately two feet by one foot in size, piled up on the floor. We ripped one of them open to see what was inside. It was full of brand-new leather handbags, roughly twenty to a carton.

We could easily sell these bags for a few grand, but this was a drop in the ocean. Our problem was where to put them. We shone our torches to see what was around us and saw, in the left-hand corner, a staircase that went up to a large square alcove. Perfect to fit the boxes into.

KP found the electricity source and switched it on, saving us having to call out WD and waste precious time. We unloaded the backdrops from the motor then blacked out the windows on the ground level, which took an hour. The building could hold two to three thousand on each floor, and was clean and didn't need tidying up.

We ran out of backdrops so the windows upstairs had to be spray-painted to stop the morning light spoiling our special effects. Telephoning the equipment crew, we instructed them to drive to the warehouse loading-dock. Within five minutes, two sets of headlights approached the entrance, which we quickly opened, and once they were inside the gates were padlocked with locks and chains. Nobody was allowed to leave the building until all the work was completed.

We fixed the projectors to the walls along with strobe arc lines, smoke machines and fan lights. The sound system had 5k upstairs and 5k downstairs, with two different rigs and DJ consoles with double decks, all supplied by a guy called Hans who had loads of equipment and access to as much as we could possibly use.

The reception area was perfect to use as an entrance to the party, and the warehouse office was turned into a command centre. I'd become accustomed to our makeshift HQs but it still gave me a buzz to stand in this room. The mobile phones and walkie-talkies on the table were our lifeline to the rest of the country and thousands of prospective punters. This bunker and nerve centre of our whole operation kept us two steps ahead of law enforcement and informers.

The phones soon sprang to life with a constant flow of callers who were itching for any information regarding a meeting point or the plot in general. We had loads of money bags, binliners and clipboards, together with accounts balance sheets, which we ticked off as we made each payment to staff or for equipment hired.

Our meeting point was around five miles from the venue and had to be big enough for us not to disturb the traffic flow in the area. Sometimes we had no choice but to use selected landmarks on main roads. This point wasn't the best of meets, but was a well-known building. Our parties were always due to start at the same time each week and invariably an hour before opening we'd get a phone call from a punter telling us there were 2,000 people at the point.

Luckily for us, by now we could transform every venue we entered at lightning speed. Within hours we were just adding the finishing touches. One of our staff arrived at the meeting point just as five police vans pulled up, and telephoned me on a direct private line to let me know what was occurring. I told him to send the party people down.

A flick of a switch brought our creation to life, and the high-tech dance arena looked like a vision of the future. I felt an incredible rush, and goose pimples did a Mexican wave across my body and over my scalp. Life was fantastic! We were 22 years old, with bundles of cash, loads of personality, untold women, and infamous throughout the club scene. In a material sense, life couldn't be better. We were only young, and had earned the respect of the whole entertainment industry, from club owners to concert promoters.

Hundreds of cars were screeching to a halt and parking outside the warehouse. Security quickly got as many people inside as was humanly possible. Our meeting-point man telephoned to say that Dibble was following the convoy, so I waited in anticipation and worked out what bullshit story to spin them this time.

A punter told me that the police had blocked the whole entrance road to the industrial estate, and I told Tony I'd handle this one alone. I took with me my telephone, a walkie-talkie, a moody guest list, a clipboard and a snide lease. The police had already blocked both slip roads off the A406. I couldn't see a flat-cap so I approached the nearest plodder.

'What on Earth do you think you're doing?' I asked.

'Are you in charge of all this, then?' Dibble replied.

'My name is Michael Mifsud and I'm George Michael's personal manager. I strongly suggest that you move your vehicles, or else I'll be forced to telephone my lawyer.'

'Look, just calm down. I don't want to have to arrest you on public disorder charges,' he said.

'Arrest me? Do you think I'm stupid? I have every right to be on this property and have the written permission of the owner. If you cannot authorise the dispersing of this roadblock, you had better bring me someone that can. And please let me inform you that every minute you waste in contacting whoever you need to speak to will be added to an account of events, structured by myself and handed to our legal department.'

With this warning, I gave him the snide lease. The copper glanced at it, then walked over to his colleagues and conferred with them. I got on the walkie-talkie and told them to send some workers up to the main road to direct the cars to another part of the estate, two minutes up the road. Punters could park there and walk to the venue. Dibble returned to me and said he couldn't do anything until the chief of police arrived. In retaliation, I asked whether he realised he wasn't dealing with a bunch of amateurs and that his job was on the line. For good measure, I also noted his name and number.

Scores of people were turning up on foot by now and so I directed them to the warehouse. The police didn't stop anyone from walking past their cars. They were only interested in blocking cars from entering the estate. Then the clouds opened up and dropped a ton of water on our heads, which, in addition to a freezing-cold wind, made life most unpleasant as I stood there in my shirt and tie.

Every party we threw, we had a walkie-talkie code word that would indicate that something secret was about to be said. This party's code was 'What time are the limos arriving?' On hearing this, I walked away from Dibble and replied 'All clear.' Only when I repeated this code would the person on the other end of the walkie-talkie give me the important message.

I was told that there were already 2,000 people in the warehouse. I asked for an umbrella and some charlie to be brought out to me. The A406 was by now almost at a standstill in both directions and police sirens broke the silence of the night. I knew that all those reinforcements were coming to us and butterflies flapped inside my ribcage. Four police vans and three cars came speeding around the bend and stopped by the other vehicles. Eight or nine uniforms jumped out of each van and plenty more out of the motors. In the middle of them all was a flat-cap, the big chief, the guvna, numero uno, top of the heap, the don, him upstairs, da boss, king of the beasts.

Flanked by a sea of blue, the top man walked straight up to me. I took a deep breath, put on my best posh voice and firmly shook his hand. Another officer handed him the lease and suddenly I was completely surrounded by around 40 policemen who were all glaring aggressively right at me. Now, I'd dealt with groups of ten officers before and handled that perfectly, but this was different. Very different.

'My officers have informed me of what was said to them earlier,' he said, 'and I have to say that I'm not entirely happy with what's going on here.'

'No, no, no! Please let me inform you, sir, that I am George Michael's personal manager. This private party is in celebration of a new single and video that will be released next month. We have giant video screens erected that will exclusively show the new video to members of the entertainment industry.'

'Yes, but do you have any proof of your status?' he asked. 'Why should I take this claim at face value?'

'I am a very busy man, sir. If you choose not to believe me, then it is down to you to prove that I'm an imposter. I have 3,000 especially invited guests from the music industry to contend with. There are ten major stars inside right now, including George Michael and Elton John. If you, alone, would care to accompany me and meet them, I'm sure they'd have a lot to say to you. Bearing in mind that you are obstructing his personal guests and causing them discomfort, George isn't exactly going to be very happy.'

I presented the chief with the moody guest list, which was the same one we'd used on several occasions. It contained about 200 celebrity names, with some of them crossed off as if they'd already arrived.

'The point is, officer, your roadblock is turning our most important guests away. All of this area here is reserved for their limos. Now, can you please disperse your blockade and let us do our job as smoothly as possible, without any hiccoughs or law suits? We'll be out of your hair before you know it.'

The chief stood in thought for a moment, then said, 'OK, fine. I am satisfied this is a private event. In future, if you plan on organising anything like this in my area again, you must arrange it with my station beforehand. Do we understand one another?'

'Loud and clear, sir. Now, do you mind moving these cars?'

The inspector instructed his men to open the blockade and they jumped back into their vehicles and drove off, leaving six policemen behind. The cars immediately came pouring in and began parking everywhere. Although it was raining, our guests were all smiling and saying 'Hello' to me. Many of them had seen me with policemen on previous occasions and knew that what I was doing was essential for the continuation of the party. They'd be on their best behaviour when walking past the law.

One of the policemen asked me if I would like him to direct the traffic and help the people parking. Ha! I said I'd be grateful for any help he could give me. Then he asked me what other celebrities would be arriving that night. I asked him if he liked Mandy Smith and his eyes and mouth pinged open. I said she would be arriving within the next couple of hours, and he asked if he could get her autograph. I told him I'd do better than that: I'd introduce him to her. Of course she wasn't coming, but at least it kept him buzzing for a few hours!

I'd told so many lies that night that I thought it would be best if I stayed outside with the police. The charlie got me paranoid and I began to think that if I let somebody else man this area, they might blow my cover. The E I'd taken was also complicating matters! But I didn't mind being there: I was having quite a good laugh with Dibble. Old Bill were OK and didn't give a toss about our party. If it were down to them, they'd be out catching real crooks.

Suddenly a voice crackled over the walkie-talkie, saying the emergency code words: 'Have the limos arrived yet?'

'All clear.'

'Listen, we've got a slight problem. You'd better come over straight away,' said Dick, one of our security men.

'No, I can't leave my position. What's up?'

'I'll come and talk to you in person. I'll be with you in a second.'

Dick stood about 6 feet tall by 4 feet wide. He'd been a hired mercenary who had fought in most of the covert and revolutionary wars spanning the previous ten years and the stories he could tell would frighten the living daylights out of you. This guy was a trained killer who had worked for some very influential people. I reckon Dick could kill a person in a hundred different ways using only one finger. He used to do that move that Spock from *Star Trek* does to render an undesirable unconscious. He'd done it to some people at Leaside Road when we'd had some trouble with a few drunks who didn't understand the concept of dance parties.

These geezers had thought the loved-up punters were poofs or something, so they'd gone all out to start a fight. Rather than kicking their heads in and throwing them out on the street, which usually happens in pubs and clubs, our security team ran up to them and gently touched their shoulder area. They simply fell in a heap on the floor. The security guys then chucked the stunned bodies over their shoulders and took them around the comer. They came to minutes later, sitting down leaning against a wall, suffering from shock. They never came back to the party, though, and after an experience like that neither would I, mate. Yet our door policy wasn't about bashing people up: that went against everything we believed in.

I looked down the dimly lit road towards the venue, which you couldn't see from where we were standing because of buildings obscuring the view. Dick stepped out from the dark road and I walked over to him. He was a very thorough and decisive man who'd always get straight to the point, diagnose the problem and give you several solutions. He was a very angry person who had learnt to control and manipulate his temper to use it for his own ends. He had a thirteen-stone Rottweiler that he always brought to work with him. If it hadn't been for his giant size you probably wouldn't feel intimidated by him at all. Even with his huge build, you might say he was a gentle giant. But this guy had the capability to top anybody in the blink of an eye.

'There's a geezer back there, standing in the reception, claiming this is his venue because he saw it first. He's got a pit bull terrier with him and is wearing a raincoat with one hand in his pocket. I can't tell if he's got a firearm or not. He says he's not leaving until we give him some money or he's gonna 'ave it with us. He's got a bagful of fliers advertising a party here next week. I've calmed him down a bit but he's still there. Is there any way he could have found out last week where you were having this party, or is he trying it on?' asked Dick.

'No, there's no way,' I replied. 'Only three of us knew.'

'Well, the only reason we haven't taken him out yet is so we could talk to you first,' said Dick. 'If you don't want to give him anything or discuss this any further, I'll just say the word. Everyone is ready to steam him. He's got balls though, to walk up to ten blokes standing in the reception and demand money with menaces! What I'm trying to say,' continued Dick, 'is that if we're going to do him, then I suggest we do it properly. We'll steam him, put him in the motor, take him to a plot and put one in the back of his head. Geezers like him don't just disappear. He'll be back some time, so we may as well deal with it now and it's done. At the end of the day, I don't want to be standing on that door when he turns up with a shooter. I'd rather top him now. It's down to you: I'll deal with it any way you want.'

I stood deep in thought, pondering my reply. 'OK, I don't want a mini-war on our hands,' I said. 'If his flyers look authentic and if the others agree, give him £500. I'm not doing these parties to kill or be killed. If he's not happy with our offer, call me on the walkie-talkie. I've blagged these parties and I'm going to do them for a good while longer.'

'OK, whatever you say. I'll shout you on the walkie-talkie.'

Until Dick spoke to me I had been on a high, and rightly so. The party was rammed with 6,000 people having the time of their lives. I knew I could never live with the knowledge that I had authorised someone being killed simply because they'd believed we'd nicked their gaff. In fact, our own boys would be doing exactly what he was doing, if we found ourselves on the other side of the equation. This geezer was carrying flyers with the warehouse address printed on. He certainly couldn't have known we were planning to use the place. And even if I'd thought he was pulling a fast one, I wouldn't have wanted him killed or anything as extreme as that, simply ejected from the premises.

It was still raining and really cold and I was only wearing a suit and raincoat. I was very pissed off. The policemen were being very helpful, however. By now they were my pals and could tell I was no hardened criminal, just a young entrepreneur trying to make a living in a Thatcherite society. The Old Bill were still waiting for their celebrity autographs, however, so I said Mandy Smith's limo driver must have taken another route to the warehouse.

Dick called over the radio and told me the intruder had accepted our offer and was no longer on the premises. Deciding it was time to go inside, I made my excuses and returned to the venue. A cheer went up as I stepped into the reception: the security were in high spirits and so was Teena, who was taking the money.

The ground level was bursting with energy and people were jumping up and down while the DJ played an awesome set. I made my way through the sea of dancing bodies where people were hugging one another and projecting love and harmony. I stopped in front of the DJ console where Keith, KP and the lads were going for it, gave a thumbs-up sign to the DJ and started to get down. One of my all-time favourites was in the mix: 'Let The Music Use You' by Frankie Knuckles. This tune was big and guaranteed to move the crowd to total ecstasy. The whole venue sang along:

This song is from my heart.
It wasn't easy from the start.
Say, can't you see, everybody is dancing with me?
So let the music use you.

This record does something to my heartstrings even now: it's the absolute bollocks. Looking around the warehouse, at the far end of the building, amongst the smoke, I could see a single green light, and I headed towards this starlight glow. Somehow, the nearer I got, the further away the light seemed to be. All around me I could hear voices talking about this fascinating aura that couldn't be reached. I continued my mission to catch this light and began running towards the wall until WHAM! The solid wall remained firm, and I bounced off the concrete bricks and hit the floor!

Somebody was holding my arm. I tried to open my eyes, but they wouldn't react and I could barely see through the slit of my eyelashes. Suddenly green hands were everywhere and trying to pin me down. I grabbed hold of the nearest fingers and sank my teeth into them. There was a loud scream straight away.

When my eyes opened fully, I saw loads of people wearing bandanas and smiley faces telling me to let go of the hand I had in my mouth! I released my locked jaw and was helped to my feet.

Shaking my head, I said, 'What the fuck was that?'

One geezer said, 'Not to worry, I've been standing here an hour and seen at least 10 people do the same thing. My eyes are hurting because I've been staring at it for such a long time.'

I apologised to the guy whose hand I'd bitten and asked if he was OK. I must have bitten him hard because he had prominent teeth marks on the back of his hand, between his forefinger and thumb. I got some money out of my pocket, gave him a fifty and sent him to our on-site paramedic, Charlise.

Charlise was a fully qualified nurse who loved to party and understood the Ecstasy rush because she'd been there herself, many a time. She'd normally take the casualty out into the fresh air, sit them down and talk them through the overwhelming rush they were experiencing. If it was more serious she was even prepared to take patients to hospital and stay with them until they were given the all clear, although we'd never had to go to these extremes. Charlise was worth her weight in gold and of great value to the team: it made us feel a lot more secure to have a paramedic on site.

The warehouse was still rammed at 10 a.m. but enough was enough and it was time to close: we knew we shouldn't push our luck too far. Keith and Tony went to the safe house to split the money and I planned to meet them later that night after some well-deserved kip. I'd been awake for two days and was in urgent need of some rest. So once everybody had left the building and was safely on their way, I let the security go home. I had arranged for a couple of mates to keep watch on all the equipment in the warehouse and so had to wait half an hour for the duo to arrive.

Changing into jeans, Timberlands, jumper, padded jacket and a Stussy cap, I felt a lot warmer. Lack of sleep and too many class-A substances were beginning to take their toll. I felt a bad cold coming on and knew my health was about to deteriorate rapidly. I sat on a dance podium with a parachute wrapped around my shoulders for the extra heat and took a bag of charlie from out my pocket. Sticking a fifty pence into the bag, I snorted the pile up one nostril, then repeated the process and did the other side.

Suddenly, the tranquil silence of the old building was shattered by the sound of an over-revving van. A police van with its headlights on full-beam was heading towards me. I slowly got up and stepped off the platform, leaving the gear wrapped in the shiny parachute material. Behind the van was a marked police car and three or four officers running on foot.

The police took firm hold of each of my arms and said that I was under arrest. I asked them what grounds they had and was told breaking and entering for a start, and that by the time we got to the station they'd have thought of a few more charges. I told them I was a rigger waiting for the equipment vans to turn up and that none of the stuff was mine: it belonged to my boss, who was at home sleeping. Dibble said that everything in the building was being confiscated and taken into police storage. If a receipt was produced for each item, the equipment would be returned. They arrested me, together with KP. I was taken to the local station, which I figured must be where the chief and squad from the previous night were based.

Suddenly I felt very vulnerable. Here I stood, in a police charge room, surrounded by untold plodders who had somehow discovered the truth about the venue. I wasn't about to start shouting my mouth off, telling them I was the organiser and they had no right to hold me. Fuck that! I stuck to my story: I was a rigger, I worked helping the lighting and sound technicians attach fixtures to the walls and I was promised £25 for a few hours' work. One of the Old Bill asked me if it was true that the DJs earned ten grand a night, and I said I could guarantee him that no DJ in the country was asking or getting that kind of money. Dibble clearly thought that the DJs controlled the parties and made all the wonger! I played ignorant and said that I really didn't know.

The police locked me in a cell for ten hours, which I spent worrying whether the evening shift of Old Bill would be the same coppers as had been on duty the night before. If it was, I would be in deep shit, and I panicked internally at the thought of being made a scapegoat and given a prison sentence to warn off other promoters. I hoped I wouldn't get recognised. How could I have been so stupid? Why the fuck did I stay in the warehouse in the first place?

In the evening the heavy steel door unlocked and opened.

'This way please,' said a plodder, pointing towards the charge room.

I immediately noticed that the desk sergeant wasn't the same one as earlier. Shit! The shifts had indeed changed! The room was very lively with loads of officers standing around chatting to one another, so I stared at the floor, not wanting to make eye contact with anyone. The desk sergeant informed me they weren't pressing charges, and I was free to go. He was just in the process of handing back my possessions when the flat-cap I had successfully blagged the night before walked into the room. Trying to make a quick exit, as I reached the door I heard the chief's voice.

'Excuse me, don't I know you?' he said.

'Who, me? I doubt it. I'm not from this area.'

'What's your name?' he asked.

'George Norman.'

'So, are you going to do any more parties in this area?'

'I couldn't tell you. I'm only a rigger.'

'Well, can you please advise the organisers that we are on full alert and will not tolerate a gathering of this kind again? If you do return to any local industrial estates, you'll be met by a riot squad. Am I making myself clear?' he asked.

'I don't know them personally. I'll tell my boss, and he'll give them your message.'

'Yes, you do that. Now get out of here, and don't come back.'

'Goodbye, and thank you,' I said.

Keith picked me up and we drove to meet Tony and a bunch of lads. They bought me a crate of champagne and an ounce of sniff to soothe away the blues. When I told them I hadn't been charged because they thought I was a rigger we rolled about laughing for hours: 'Top fucking blag, mate!'

We stayed up all night (as you do) talking about ways in which we could get a licensed legal warehouse, or even a later club licence, which would only bring us in line with the rest of Europe. The licensing conditions in England were positively medieval and were in urgent need of review. To have an 8 a.m. licence application granted to dance-party promoters was nigh on impossible. Not only that: property owners who leased us their buildings were threatened with imprisonment or the loss of their licence. A stern warning was given to landowners who even dared think of giving us the use of their property.

What chance did we have against a government that didn't understand what was going on? The Acid House dream wasn't just about getting fucked off your tits in a disused warehouse. We were the children of the future who had found our direction. The dominating factor that would propel us into the next millennium was that all races would face this chapter together. The old-school patterns of thought would be replaced by a new-found unity. So we sat and joked about organising a demonstration in the centre of London on a Saturday afternoon: 20,000 people marching through Oxford Street demanding their rights as citizens to party all night long.

As it turned out, this was to be our last event with Sunrise. Tony went on to arrange legal parties in equestrian centres around the country. This was inevitable: Sunrise didn't need us, and we didn't need them. We were all good friends and had the most respect for one another. Meanwhile, we hit the road in search of a suitable warehouse.

GENESIS 1989: CHAPTER OF CHAPTERS

Things were starting to get a bit hot for us. The police had been duped on several occasions and it wouldn't be long before they caught on. We knew we had to form a decisive plan of action that ensured that in future our parties couldn't be stopped. Our first decision was to locate at least two venues so that, in the event of an emergency, we could swap warehouses. We could hire enough equipment to stock both gaffs, and have two teams at the ready to complete the job. It was worth the double costs to ensure our peace of mind.

Our first week of searching afresh was very productive. Within a couple of days, we'd found two buildings. One was off an A road in north London and was the last warehouse down the end of a private road. A huge enclosed yard went around the building and could hold a hundred or so motors.

We were trying to look inside the warehouse when a voice close behind us said, 'Can I help you?'

We turned around to see a man on a bike pedalling out of a small metal gateway that led to a river. We asked the geezer whether he knew who owned the building but he didn't, and pointed to a caravan parked further up the road. We walked towards the caravan and a scruffy security guard came out to meet us.

'Excuse me, I wonder if you can tell us who owns this building?' I said.

'I'm sorry, I can't help you there,' he answered. 'It's been empty for over a year and nobody goes in or out.'

I felt my pulse quickening. 'Look, can we be straight with you?'

'Yeah!'

'We organise special music business parties in ware-houses like this and we're looking for a venue to stage our next show. If we were to give you £100 to turn a blind eye on Saturday next week, what would your reaction be?'

'Oh, I'm not sure about that, mate. I might get into trouble. You'll have to speak to Martin first.'

'Who's Martin?'

'He lives on one of those houseboats down there –' he pointed to the gates '– and he speaks for everyone along this stretch of river.'

'Can you introduce us to him?' asked Keith. 'If you both agree with our plan, we'll give you the money up front.'

The geezer took us through the gate and towards a shabby-looking houseboat that looked virtually incapable of staying afloat. The guard shouted, and after a couple of minutes a head popped out of the wooden entrance to the floating nightmare and asked us to climb aboard.

Surprisingly, the interior was clean, decorated in quite a bohemian style, and looked comfortable. There were giant cushions on the floor, ornaments from India on the shelves, and the smell of incense filled the air. Ambient melodies played on a small cassette player in the background.

Martin was the absolute image of a Sixties hippie, a man who was totally in touch with the world and at one in his heart, tall, dark-haired and softly spoken. He introduced us to his girlfriend and motioned for us to sit down on one of the big cushions. On the table in front of us was a huge bong. We've always been puffers and had draw on us nearly all of the time. We pulled blocks of hash from each of our pockets and put them on the table. As Martin began preparing the home-made water bong, we explained what we had planned for the warehouse and said that we expected around a thousand people. Martin thought it was a fantastic idea and was right up for it. The only problem he thought we'd have was that the other boat owners might not like the noise and hassle. Keith and I suggested that we should pay for everyone to go away for the weekend and Martin's eyes lit up.

'Yeah, that would be cool,' he said.

There were nine other houseboats moored together and we said we'd give each owner £200 towards a weekend break. If Martin could make the arrangements we'd give him a monkey and, as soon as we got the all clear, he'd get the money. Martin asked us if we'd seen the building's interior and said that he'd show it to us – but not before a hit from his well-packed bong.

Once we got to the warehouse, a single doorway led inside. Martin booted the door and it immediately swung open. Wow! This was fantastic! What a pukka venue! The place was the size of six full-size football pitches and the ceiling just went up and up, perfect for a full-on lighting show. This was definitely the best gaff we'd ever seen. Our punters were going to love what we had in store for them.

Keith and I thanked Martin for his time and said that we'd return with everybody's money in a couple of days. We drove away screaming and shouting: we knew that this was the one that would guarantee our name in the dance-party hall of fame. This party would put us on the very top of the world map of party events.

We returned to the houseboat two days later with the money that we had promised the owners. Martin was very happy: we must have seemed like two wise men bearing gifts! But little did he know what lay ahead. We'd told him that a thousand people were coming, but really we expected at least six times that number. The venue could comfortably hold 8,000 party people just on one level. We were so excited about our new warehouse that we forgot to check the electric fuse box to see if it was operational …

We printed a thousand flyers and decided to record a special 40-second radio commercial for the pirate stations. I used the anthem 'Pacific State' as a soundtrack and we recorded it at Noise Gate Studios in south east

London. I wrote a script and presented it to the studio's voiceover specialist, but wasn't happy with the result and asked him to put a bit more life into his voice. Insulted by this request, he replied that I should do it myself if I thought I could do better!

I'd never spoken into a microphone before so I felt embarrassed, but grabbed the mike and gave it a crack. My chosen backing track always conjured up great memories, so in a slow and clear voice I started to read from my hand-written script:

In a secret location, somewhere in London, Genesis '89 proudly presents the Chapter of Chapters.

An invitation to all Genesis members and veterans. Entertainment will be supplied by an all-star DJ line-up, including: Fabio, Grooverider, Mickey Finn, Tony Wilson, Dem 2 and Bones.

A production of the highest quality includes 60k of turbo-sound, lasers, special effects and cinematic-sized projections.

For the information hotline, please stay tuned. Genesis '89 is live and kicking.

This only took one take but I knew it was perfect. I could feel every word. Even the voiceover guy had to admit the playback sounded the nuts, pure class. I discovered a new talent that day, and have since recorded around 70 professional radio commercials – a nice little sideline!

We went all out to promote this event through every avenue open to us, including Camden Palace, Heaven, Astoria, Shoom and small parties around town. We placed flyers in record and clothes shops. Promotion wasn't very hard because everyone had heard of the party and wanted to attend anyway.

On party night, we arrived at the warehouse by 5 p.m. as usual, with two vans of equipment following us. We drove on to the private road alongside the river, which led straight into the warehouse yard. Keith went into the entrance and opened the large loading-bay shutter. It was only then that we realised the electricity source hadn't been checked.

We hunted down the fuse box and found it smashed to bits, with all the fuses missing! Fuck, fuck, fuck, how did we forget that?! We got WD, our sparks, on the blower and fortunately found him at home, but he lived on the other side of the water. It would take him at least 45 minutes to reach us. There was nothing we could do but wait in the hope that he could fix our problem.

During the previous week I'd met a guy who owned a lighting company and had two lasers for hire. Nobody I knew of had used lasers in a warehouse before so I had booked him for the weekend. Lasers added a new dimension and created fantastic special effects in a nightclub. Imagine the atmosphere this could generate in a huge warehouse full of people! Top fucking buzz, mate!

The electricity not being on was an obvious sign of something being wrong. The laser geezer turned up, quickly sussed this and wanted to leave straight away. Fortunately, I persuaded him to stay by promising him an extra £500. If the laser got confiscated, I told him, all he had to do was produce a receipt and collect the equipment from the nearest police station. If Dibble wouldn't give it back, we'd pay for the fucker. Twenty grand? Sweet, he'd have it by the morning.

We always carried a float of five grand or more, just in case the gig got stopped. Certain people still had to get paid – this was their bread and butter – and just because we'd lost out didn't mean everyone else should. Five jib would keep them quiet until Monday, but if we didn't have any money at all there'd be a scream up. I gave him £1,800 for one night's rental, which was a lot, but what the hell – we had fucking lasers!

To break the tension of impatiently awaiting the arrival of WD, I turned the car stereo on. The first tune was 'Can You Feel It?' by Fingers Inc., which included the famous Martin Luther King words: 'I have a dream'. These words sank into my heart: we felt like we were living out our biggest dream of all. We didn't have to worry about Old Bill turning up because the night watchman had taken a bung of a bottle of whisky and had a walkie-talkie to alert us if anyone approached the road. We knew we could make as much noise as we wanted. The next track was 'I need a little bit, got to have a little bit, I need a little bit, of respect' – a wicked tune, man! Our phones were off, and for a brief moment I found myself lost in music.

Somebody started banging on the door and we quickly switched the music off. I called the night watchman on the walkie-talkie and he told me that he'd been calling for five minutes trying to tell me that a black guy in a red car had pulled into the yard. Phew! It was WD.

I ran around to open the door and straight away showed him the fuse box. WD said it was so bad he wasn't sure it could be fixed, but he would do his best to sort it. Time was running out: it was 6.20 p.m. We needed to start setting the equipment up, despite having no lights or power.

I decided that we should start the engines on all the cars: I figured that the full headlight beams of all the vehicles lined up together was better than nothing. I'd give everybody petrol money to compensate later, and at least this way their car batteries wouldn't run down. While the lads set things up, I got on the phone and called our back-up crew. Their equipment wasn't up to our usual standards but they could do the job at a push. The big advantage of our back-up crew was that they didn't give a fuck about a venue being illegal; all we had to do was to tell them where it was. They'd break into it themselves, and quickly do the business. As long as we gave them a wage, they'd do anything.

The stand-by warehouse we'd prepared for this evening had electricity and wasn't too far away, but was a bit complicated to find, so we knew we'd have to recruit guides to lead people to the location. It also only had the capacity to hold 2,000 people, which would definitely cause chaos in the surrounding area. This was why we had kept it purely as a back-up venue, only for use in extreme emergencies.

I told the boys to hit the road and head towards the substitute venue and phone me once they got there, then went to see how WD was getting on. He said the fuse box still looked pretty bad, but could be fixed if he went to pick up some parts from a friend's place in south London. By then it was 7 p.m. and, in another two hours, thousands would be at the meeting point, five minutes down the road. We had to act fast. The nearest street lamp was a long way down the road and we knew that if we got wired up to that lamp we'd be spotted straight away. WD promised it wouldn't take him more than an hour to go and return with the missing parts, and it wouldn't be long after that before full electricity would be restored. Quickly making an exit, he was on his way.

The equipment crew, meanwhile, was doing very well and most of their equipment was already in place. We didn't have a ladder high enough to reach the ceiling, so a lot of the lights were attached to side walls. The laser would fill the top half of the venue with its green and blue beams and just needed to be plugged in. Martin walked in and called us over: he had his bong filled up ready to be smoked. We had a hit, thanked him, then returned to facing our stress and pure worry.

I took stock of our situation. We were standing in a warehouse with no fucking electricity, with one-and-a-half hours to get organised before thousands of people congregated at the meeting point. Not only that, but this gaff was only ten minutes away from the one we used when I got nicked, so there was a very strong possibility that the area would be governed by the same police chief. If *he* turned up, it would quite certainly be all over for me.

'Wayne, the guy in the red car is driving into the yard,' said the watchman's voice over the walkie-talkie.

'Yes! It's WD!' yelled KP.

Our sparky came running through with fuses in hand, stuck them into their slots, and the lights came on. The adrenaline spread from my brain and filled my tired soul with energy. My promoter's nerves had all but disappeared: our pre-designed Twilight Zone was taking shape. The lasers were plugged in and went through their special effect routines and looked amazing. This was really going to set pulses racing!

'Wayne! Emergency, emergency! Two police cars are heading your way,' crackled the radio.

'Listen up, everyone, Old Bill is here,' I said. 'Here's the story: this is a film shoot for TV. You don't have to say anything apart from that. If they ask questions, send them to me. This is just a precaution.'

I walked over to the warehouse shutters and began to open them. As I did so, three policemen stepped underneath the barrier. The main lighting was off and the lasers and lights were on. Before I could say a word, one of the officers commented on how fantastic the lights looked, and walked into a position where he could get a better view.

'Who are you, and who's in charge?' asked one of the officers.

An inner voice told me to tell them my real name.

'Hi, I'm Wayne Anthony from Channel Four Films. It's my responsibility to manage and maintain this site. The head of Youth Programming is Janet Street-Porter: she's my boss,' I replied.

'Oh really? The one who did that programme years ago, on Sundays?' he asked.

'Yeah, that's her. She's come a long way since those days. She manages most of the programmes on Channel Four now.'

'So where are the cameras?' he asked me.

'The camera equipment and production team is arriving within the next three hours. For the moment, we're just finishing the set.'

'Our chief will be here shortly,' he informed me. 'Tell him what you've told us, and everything will be fine. The lighting show looks great. How long has all this stuff taken to put up?'

'The lighting and sound technicians have been here all week. Now, I hope you don't think I'm being rude but I have some work to be getting on with. Please feel free to look around the building.'

I went back to the main entrance, where Keith was talking with WD. Telephoning the back-up crew, I checked how things were going at the other warehouse. They only had to attach some lights and position the sound system; we didn't expect them to clear away the rubbish as well. It was only 8.15 p.m. and already hundreds of people were gathering at the point, so I sent someone there immediately.

Flashing lights stopped in front of the shutters, car doors slammed shut and in walked a flat-cap flanked by ten plodders. The main lighting was now on and the full extent of our work was on display. As I made my way across the warehouse, I heard one of the policemen tell the chief what a fantastic light show we had. Before I could say a word, the same officer asked me to show his boss the special effects. I called for someone to hit the light switch and the laser beams pierced the dark warehouse interior and went into one of their programmed routines.

'Are you doing that on purpose?' the police chief asked.

'Doing what, exactly?'

'Switch the main lights on immediately!' he replied.

I did.

'Who are you, and what are you doing here?' the inspector asked me.

'My name is Wayne Anthony. I'm special projects manager for Channel Four Films. We're going to be filming a scene for use in a future film production to be screened on Channel Four.'

'A film for Channel Four? Where are the cameras?'

'The production team arrives at midnight. We're shooting the entire scene with steadicams to allow us full interaction with the extras on the ground.'

'Do you have paperwork to that effect?'

'I have a copy of the lease relating to use of the venue, but the production contracts are at the office.'

I handed the police chief the Mickey Mouse document.

'Would you mind stepping outside, please, sir?' the chief asked me.

'Is there a problem? Do you realise you are standing on private property?' I asked in a stern voice.

'You are not under arrest, sir. I would merely like a private talk with you alone and not with your entire crew.'

I agreed, and led the inspector out of the entrance and into the yard. There were around 400 people standing in a neat line against the warehouse wall. Everybody went quiet as we walked through the door and over to a perimeter fence, where we couldn't be heard.

'What did you say your full name and address were?' he grilled me.

'My name is Wayne Anthony and please don't try to play games with me,' I bluffed. 'Your intimidation tactics won't work. If you have a problem, then let's hear it. My legal department will rip you to shreds. I don't have the time or the patience to play your childish games.'

'Now look here, Wayne, I'm not stupid. You're not from Channel Four and there's no filming happening here tonight. Before you say anything, I know exactly what's going on and how much money is involved. Are you telling me my information is wrong, Wayne?'

'You are as far from the truth as we are from the beach,' I said. 'I can see we're going to have a problem here so I'm calling my lawyer. You have no idea what you are starting. My company is represented by some of the best law companies in the world.'

'I find you very cocky and irritating, young man,' said the inspector. 'I'm trying to solve this situation as best I can. Don't threaten me like some common constable. I could be the biggest spanner in the works you've ever encountered.'

'I am from Channel Four,' I repeated, slowly. 'We are shooting a scene for a TV movie. You've seen the hire lease, and everything is in order. My cocky and irritating attitude, as you call it, derives from representing a powerful company, who will not take kindly to a paranoid and interfering police chief. I respect you and the law you stand for, but please go and play with somebody else.'

'OK, Wayne, is there anyone standing in that queue of people who could confirm your name to me?' he asked me.

I looked at all the people waiting to be let inside and scanned the faces, trying to find somebody that I knew. A mate of mine from the East End was halfway down the line and I called him over.

'Crimble! Everything's all right, mate. Can you do me a favour and tell this police inspector my name?' I asked.

'Nah, sorry, I don't wanna get involved,' he said.

'Honest, it's sweet, bruv! If you don't tell him, he's going to stop the shoot.'

Crimble looked at me for a sign. I nodded.

'I think it's Wayne something,' he said. 'Wayne Anthony. Can I go now?'

'Cheers, mate. Go straight to the front. I'll see you in a minute.'

'How many people do you expect tonight?' the inspector demanded.

'We have 800 extras plus a crew of a hundred.'

'Let me inform you, Mr Anthony, the time is now 9 p.m. I will leave, and return at 11p.m. with a full riot squad. If there are any more than 900 people here you will be held personally responsible and promptly escorted to a warm cell to await charges. I don't like you, or what you represent. If I find any untruths in what you've told me I shall see to it that you serve a prison sentence. Believe me, I know a lot more judges than you do.'

The police chief signalled to the other officers that they should clear out. Yes! It was party time! I phoned the point man and told him to give everyone directions: I knew thousands of people were already there. Our command centre upstairs was operational, and the warehouse looked the nuts.

The DJ hadn't shown up yet so there was no music, but KP had his record box in the boot of my car so I rushed out to get it. I brought the box inside and tried to get someone to play the tunes, but everyone bottled it. Now, I've always been into music but never at any time wanted to be a DJ: the business of music and promoting is my thing.

The warehouse was quickly filling up: there were about 3,000 people already, and no fucking DJ. A small crowd started clapping and within minutes the whole place echoed with people putting their hands together. Then the legendary chant could be heard: 'Aceeed, Aceeed, Aceeed'. It was clear that I had to do something pronto.

Nervously, I went to the decks, put the box on a table and searched through its contents for a track that I recognised. My first tune was 'Real Wild House', which has a wicked piano riff. The warehouse erupted and hands shot into the air as lasers displayed an imaginative routine of effects. I had never tried mixing in my life and so simply faded the track into the next one, which was 'Seduction'. I was kicking butt, man! I could get used to this job: it's not as hard as it looks. 'Sueno Latino' was my last track before I let the DJ, Tony Balearic Wilson, take control. He mixed his first tune in perfectly. He played 'Jibro' followed by 'Flesh'.

The warehouse was nearly full, so I went up to the office and checked to see whether everything was running smoothly. It was: we had collected 60 grand already. Keith was so busy counting the money that he didn't have time to take our fortune to the safe house. The office had an *en suite* boardroom with a long, recently cleaned, wooden table where we were sorting all the wonger. A few of our mates were in the other room, sniffing out of ounce-bags of quiver.

There was a window that overlooked the yard where a load of cars were parked, and suddenly a white minibus came speeding past the window and into the last remaining tight space. He shouldn't have been there in the first place because there was meant to be someone stopping vehicles from entering the private road. This idiot might have killed someone and, unluckily for him, we had spotted him. We ran downstairs and over to the van, whose occupants were getting themselves together and jumping out of the vehicle.

'Are you fucking stupid, or something?' said Keith, grabbing the driver.

'What have I done?' he asked.

'The lot of you, get back into your van and piss off, you pricks,' screamed Keith.

'Oh, please don't, we're really sorry he drove like that. We've come all the way from Devon to be here tonight,' said one of the girls.

'I don't give a shit. He's lucky I don't do him. If he'd run someone over, what would you be saying then?' Keith argued.

I butted in. 'I'll tell you what, you lot can go in. But you can fuck off, mate, and don't come back,' I said to the driver.

'But how are we going to get home?' she asked.

'I don't care. If he doesn't start moving now, you can all go,' Keith replied.

The rest of them opted to stay and the driver got into the van and drove off. If he was smart he'd just park down the road and come back because we'd never spot him in all those faces. There must have been 2,000 people waiting to get into the warehouse by now.

I looked back up the busy private road leading to the main junction, which was crammed with motors. A traffic jam stretched as far as the eye could see. There'd been a minor crash and Keith and I made our way towards it. One car was embedded in the back of another vehicle, which turned out to belong to some of our mates, Rico, Mickey, Pondi, Gary, Rolle and Kenny, who were mad as hell.

The motorist who had crashed into them had done a runner and escaped the lads' clutches, so they'd apprehended the passengers to try to find out where the driver lived. Neither car could be pushed out of the way so we all grabbed hold of them and tried to lift them. The sound of car horns and cheers filled the air.

I glanced in the direction of the meeting point and saw the blue flashing lights of roughly ten police vans. Shit, time to go back inside! We ran like Steve Austin the bionic man back to the warehouse entrance. The Old Bill's vans were driving along the private road, weaving and dodging people as they approached the yard.

Our door takings by now amounted to 75 grand, which was packed into cardboard boxes and placed in canvas holdalls. Six security guards with shooters escorted me and Keith into the dance arena with the dash. One of our boys was outside on the walkie-talkie, monitoring Dibble. There were 8,000 party animals jumping for joy in the warehouse. We stood, feeling paranoid, near a fire exit at the back of the building, with four bags filled with money. My earphones were plugged into the walkie-talkie.

'Wayne, there's about 60 police in full combat kit approaching the door,' crackled the radio.

'I need to hear what's being said. Try to get close to them to hear what they are saying. Walk into the reception and keep the radio keyed,' I replied.

I tried to listen to what was happening, and heard the chief say, 'Where is Wayne Anthony? I want to see him immediately. This party is coming to a close.'

Fuck! We'd better get out of here, pronto, I thought. How could we get these bags of money out past Old Bill? There was a group of girls dressed in dungarees and I went over and asked if they could help us out. I suggested stuffing wads of money into their clothes, and anything else that might conceal notes. They were happy to oblige, so I took them over to my boys, who started handing over cash, which was being pushed into the girls' knickers, bras, trouser legs and hats. Keith was still listening to the radio. He said one of the doormen was pretending to look for us, and told me to listen in.

'Who's responsible for turning the music off?' asked the chief.

'Wayne is no longer on the premises,' said our guy. 'He'll be back soon.'

'Right, you'd better take us to the person in charge of the PA system. This is all over,' said the chief.

'You can't do that, mate,' said the security guard. 'This is private property. Have you got a warrant?'

'Are you taking responsibility for this fiasco?' asked the chief.

'No, I'm just stating the facts.'

'Well, I don't have to show you anything. Now take me to the source of the music before I lose my temper.'

'I'll take you to the DJ stand, but it won't do any good. Nobody will do anything without Wayne's consent: he's the boss,' said the security guy.

'We'll see about that. Let's go.'

I needed a better view of the riot squad now entering the arena and so I climbed a pipe attached to a wall. One of the security pushed open the fire exit, but it caught the attention of three policemen standing just yards away outside and so was quickly slammed shut.

By now at least 50 Old Bill were surrounding the DJ's console. I got on the radio and asked someone to check outside for a clear fire exit. At that exact moment the music stopped. Nightmare! Everyone started booing and jeering. A crowd of 300 or more began chanting 'Party, party, party' and thousands more picked up the cheer: 'PARTY, PARTY, PARTY, PARTY!' The sound bounced around the warehouse and echoed into the street like Cup Final day at Wembley.

How could they possibly stop this event? I thought. There were just too many of us. I headed for the DJ console and the army of riot police. The cry changed to 'Freedom to Party' and the whole warehouse was cheering it. The inspector knew this was a situation that could easily get out of hand and he started to move his men towards the exit. The police walked into the reception declaring that the party could continue but I would be held personally responsible. Within five minutes the police were gone and the crowd went crazy, jumping around and hugging one another.

I turned the microphone on and yelled, 'Genesis 1989!'

The DJ spun 'Meltdown' by Quartz and we all left our senses for a while. I shouted out again: 'Genesis 1989.' Everybody danced wildly with their hands in the air and began chanting: 'Genesis, Genesis, Genesis.' I looked at my partners and we screamed in each other's faces: 'Yes!' For one moment we forgot all about the security standing in the corner with 75 jib and got down to Donna Summer's 'I Feel Love'. After ten minutes we returned to the corner where even the security were boogieing – and there's no way on Earth those boys had ever danced before. The electric atmosphere had rubbed off on them and they were going for it, as were the wedged-up girls. To me, this represented a prime example of how systematically programmed minds could be reconditioned and channelled towards a brighter future.

Back in our command centre everything was running smoothly again and there was a huge queue of people outside the office. I called the lads at the back-up venue to let them know what had happened and told them to pack their stuff up and come down to us for some wages. We had already collected the bar money of about 30 grand, which was added to the boxes. The phones were going like mad and rang non-stop for hours.

A few of our friends were having a charlie session in one of the offices and Martin was with them, all loved-up and rushing from his first E. He couldn't believe how he felt or the number of people there were at the party; it reminded him of attending all the major music festivals back in the Sixties. In fact, he said it was better than Woodstock, and he'd never danced so much in his life. We sniffed some huge trench lines and a massive lump went down my throat. The buzz was so intense. Keith suggested we should take the money to Martin's boat and leave some security with it.

Then there was a knock at the door and virtually our entire security team entered the room. They asked everybody but me and Keith to leave while we had an emergency meeting.

'What's happening? Who's watching the entrance?' Keith asked.

'Listen, we need to talk about the money arrangements,' one geezer said.

'What money arrangements?'

'As we see it, we're not being paid enough money to lay our lives on the line. We've heard whispers that another AWOL army unit is planning to rob you, and they're a tough bunch of lads. They were in the Falklands the same as us, but this lot were the top unit on the force. Since then, they've been on a world tour. They arrived in England last week and they've been asking questions about us and the safe houses,' said Dick.

'So what are you saying?' asked Keith.

'It's like this,' Dick said. 'You give us 25% of the door takings instead of flat wages and we'll give you 24-hours-a-day protection against anybody that may cause you a problem. If the party gets stopped and there's no money after everything has been paid, we don't get paid. That's the deal.'

'It sounds like you're scared of the other firm,' I said.

'We're not frightened, but if we come up against the unit it will be a bloody war. We want to be sure that we're earning good money before we even think about it,' he said.

'What if we say no?' said Keith.

'We walk out now with 25% of tonight's takings and you'll be on your own. We want your decision right now, before we go any further,' he said.

I analysed our predicament. We needed a good security team, and it would have to be strong. The parties were now so big that would-be robbers knew there was some serious dosh changing hands. Although 99% of party people were fun-loving, there was always that 1% who could cause a problem. I could always recognise this minority because they'd all be standing together playing charlie big potatoes. If we didn't give Dick's team their cut, the chances were that someone else would come along and want even more. I should have knocked it on the head right there and then, but we were hooked. The huge warehouse parties, smiley faces, adrenaline rushes and colossal amounts of money were too much to resist.

Joe Public would never guess what was happening behind the scenes. We were earning illegal wonger because, in effect, the authorities had *forced* us underground. We'd tried on many occasions to hire venues through the correct channels, but as soon as we mentioned a music-business party, we got turned down flat. Nightclub licences in the late Eighties extended to 3.30 a.m. at the latest. All-night events for 8,000 people were unheard of. We wanted to play it straight at our parties and never endorsed the selling of drugs. Everybody we hired got paid. The only dodge thing we did was break into buildings and steal their electricity and, even there, if we had had a way to pay the owners they would have been sorted.

We didn't choose to be surrounded by trained killers and I hated that part of it. Their dark aura was scary shit, although some of them behaved like perfect gentlemen. Nobody ever got clumped by our security, but if it came to the crunch they'd stand up against any aspiring robbers. Yeah, it was heavy shit, but what else could you do if you were sitting on a hundred grand in an illegal venue with thousands of people around?

And now here we were, holding all this dosh with fifteen mercenaries about to take some and run. We needed these geezers, if they were as tough as they looked and acted. I was sure a test would present itself to us in the near future, although I hoped to God it didn't.

'OK, we'll agree on the condition that Genesis will always be ours to manage as we see fit,' I said. 'We don't want to know about any heavy shit – that's your department. We'll worry about organising the parties.'

'Agreed. We're glad you made the right decision. We won't let you boys down,' said Dick.

'Right, we're not being funny, but we should get this money out of here. It's making us nervous and we can take it to the boat until later,' said Keith.

He grabbed the holdalls and seven of the team escorted him to the houseboat. The party was packed solid and the bar had had to be restocked three times during that night. After this heavy and possibly life-threatening scenario, I needed to be reminded of what I was doing all this for. I went down to the dance floor and searched for the girls who had helped me to hide the wonger. I found them freaking out to 'The Dance' by Nude Photo, on the roof of a small tool shed.

I passed the bag of Peruvian flake around our new circle; one thing quickly led to another and I took them up to the command centre. A black bag of uncounted notes lay on the table so I left the girls in the adjoining room and quickly started adding up the paperwork. Then I got introduced to Chris Sullivan of The Wag Club, who told me about the warehouse parties he used to organise in the old days. Chris was most impressed with our party and its uplifting atmosphere. He told us the future of dance parties lay with promoters like us.

We split the money on the boat at 9 a.m. When we decided to go home there were 2,000 hardcore smileys still in the warehouse. I took my share of the profits and slipped off with two of the girls. The only worry now was being stopped on the way home because they would have definitely put me down as a drug dealer, with the amount of money and bag of gear I had in my possession. I didn't get to sleep that day, but it was well worth it.

KIDNAPPED!

It was a Wednesday morning and, lost in a state of semi-consciousness, I could hear banging. I wasn't sure if I was dreaming or not, when suddenly the bang turned into a crash and I jumped up thinking it was a police raid. Standing at the top of the stairs, I looked down to see three stocky geezers running up towards me.

I'd just managed to ask who they were when the first one reached me, headbutted me in the face, grabbed my throat and began punching me. I fought back but was dragged into the bedroom where all three of them were kicking, stamping and hitting me. I remember the blood gushing from my face and staining the beige carpet. What the fuck was going on?

The geezers stopped the onslaught for a few seconds to tell me that I was going for a ride, and if I made a sound when we walked out of the front door they'd top me there and then. Meanwhile, I was lying in a heap on the floor thinking my time was up and that I could do nothing to save myself. I asked them what I had done, and was told to shut the fuck up.

Bound, gagged and with a blood-soaked pillowcase over my head, I was taken outside. Their van was right outside my house. We ran across the pavement and they threw me in a sliding door on what must have been the side of the vehicle. Falling flat on my mush, I banged my shins and was smashed with what felt like an elbow. I took the blow quietly, and was thrown deeper into the van.

'If he moves, fucking shoot him!'

I heard the sound of a gun being cocked and a small single metal barrel was poked into my eye.

'If you move from this position in any fucking way, I'm gonna blow you away, do you understand?'

Nodding my head, I started to feel my body going slowly into shock. The hood was sticking to my face and I could feel the bruises and cuts throbbing through my cotton blindfold. We drove for ages along a seemingly endless motorway or A road. This is it: I'm going to die. Why me? I'm only 22. These shit cunts are all in their thirties. What have I done? All this for a few parties. Nobody even knows where I am.

I passed out and dreamt of swimming with dolphins. It felt so real that I didn't want to come back. Then somebody was carrying me and I was underwater but heard the sound of a door being opened. I crashed on to a concrete floor and the dolphins disappeared. Cold water was thrown into my masked face and woke me up like a light being switched on. It stung like mad.

A foot connected with the back of my head. A voice told me that Keith was in the room. There was a muffled noise, and the sound of knuckles against flesh. Keith and I were tied to wooden chairs and the geezers lifted our hoods only enough for them to undo the gags on our mouths. A country-bumpkin-sounding voice spoke.

'You lads don't know me, but I know a lot about you. There's two ways of doing this. You can either play tough guys, or give us what we want.'

'Who are you, and what have we done to you?' Keith said.

'Shut the fuck up,' said another country voice.

'You don't know what you're dealing with here, lads. The boys here think we should do one of you in as a lesson to the rest of you,' the first voice said.

'But we haven't done anything,' I said.

'My name is Sergeant Anderson. Has your cowboy army unit mentioned my name to you before?' asked the voice.

'No, why should they?' said Keith.

'We served in the Falklands with those pricks,' said the sergeant. 'They were tossers then, and they're tossers now. We're taking over: you lads need real looking after, not the cheap-rate services they give you. The profits are cut fifty-fifty and we'll take care of you and all the security arrangements. We had to give you a few slaps, so you'd know we're not joking. The boys here get a bit carried away sometimes.'

'We don't like Cockneys,' another voice said.

'If you don't comply with us we'll take all your money and slit your throats,' said the sergeant.

'How do we know you're not going to cut our throats anyway?' I said.

'You'll have to take my word for it. If your cowboy unit want trouble, then we'll give it them. They know how we work,' he said.

'Nah, if you're going to kill us anyway, it might as well be now,' said Keith.

'Fucking cockneys!'

They started hitting us again. They were big blokes and every blow did some damage.

'Right, give me one of your lads' telephone numbers,' said the sergeant.

'What?'

Whack! I was smacked in the head with a hard, small object – a mobile phone? I quickly said a number.

'Whose number is this?'

'It's Dick's number. It's the only one we've got.'

'What's your emergency code?' he said.

'Acid Teds.'

The tone of the keys being pressed on a phone could be heard over the sound of Keith getting a severe hiding on the other side of the room.

'Acid Teds,' said a voice, before ringing off.

The sergeant burst into laughter and the others joined in.

'That should wake them up,' one of them said. 'Fucking tossers!'

'Keith, are you all right, mate?' I asked.

'I've told you once,' one geezer said, then booted me in the chest. I fell to the ground, still tied to the chair. My head was pulled back and a thin, sharp, metal edge was pulled across my Adam's apple.

'Don't say another word,' said the geezer with the knife. The dried-up wounds on my face opened up and fresh blood poured out. I knew by now that I was in a seriously bad way. The telephone was being redialled.

'Acid Teds. Are you together yet?'

'Who the fuck are you?' I heard Dick's voice say.

'It's Sergeant Anderson, you fucking ponce.'

'Yeah, so what do you want?'

'We've got your boys here and they're a bit worse for wear. Do you want to speak to one of them?'

'What boys?'

'Dick, get us out of here,' Keith said.

'Dick, get us out of here!' laughed the sergeant. 'Well, Dick, what are you going to do? Listen, it's all over. We're here for a few months and we want a piece of the action. A big piece. Your schoolboy services have now been terminated. Do you understand?'

'I think we should have a meet,' Dick said.

'We'll meet you in Kingsbury Wood. If you can't find us, don't worry – we'll find you. You've got exactly one hour.' Click.

'Well, boys, it looks like we've got a mini-war on our hands. Ain't this great?' said another bumpkin voice.

'Let's do what we've got to do, and get out of this shite country,' said another. The sergeant began to address us. 'Now we're all going to be partners, I should apologise for the way you've been treated. We are men of honour, action and few words. I guarantee you that nobody – but nobody – will ever lay a hand on you boys again. I'm not going to remove your hoods yet, but your ordeal will be ending on a good note within the next couple of hours,' he said.

'But what about Dick and his security?' I asked.

'Don't worry. They won't give you any trouble. You have my word on it,' he said.

Keith and I were taken outside and put into the van. We drove for fifteen minutes before the vehicle screeched to a halt and we were dragged out, frogmarched into dense woodlands and tied to a tree. They threatened us with death if we made a sound. The van sped off and the forest was alive with the sound of the animal kingdom. Hours seemed to have passed before we heard branches breaking and leaves crunching.

'They're over here,' said a voice.

'Fuck me, you boys look like shit,' said Dick.

Our boys slowly removed the stiff hoods and gags, which were stuck to our cheeks, heads and mouths. I looked at Keith and saw his face was bloody and bruised. He said that I looked just as bad. We ran to our rescuers' motors and went to Keith's gaff for an urgent meeting.

Our security team told us they didn't want to tango with this firm because it would result in a massive loss of life. I asked them if they were leaving us in the hands of the sergeant and said I thought their whole purpose was to protect us and our loot. Dick simply said that the sergeant's firm were the meanest outfit in the army and would go all the way.

Keith had some charlie in the house, which Dick poured into our head wounds to numb the pain before stitching them up with a needle and cotton. We knew if we went to hospital we'd have to answer too many questions – and we didn't feel a thing, anyway. We got some women to come round with some more charlie and nurse us back to health. But our battered and bruised bodies ached for weeks.

So the 64-thousand-dollar question was: do we carry on?

Dick said that if it was any other firm than Anderson's involved, his boys would have defended our organisation to the death. He also said our attackers were a tough bunch of lads who worked really well together, so our door would be one of the strongest, if not the strongest, in the country. It was clear his earlier brave talk had been all front – he was shit-scared of Anderson. I asked him if he thought Anderson would rip us off and he said he didn't think so, but he couldn't guarantee it.

We ran the problem over in our minds. We'd worked so hard to ensure Genesis was a success and had always figured paying 25% wasn't too bad for the protection we were supposed to get. Now a bigger, badder firm wanted 50%! Where the fuck would it end? And yet, even with these calculations, we could still walk away with 30 or 40 jib from each party: a nice little earner if everything ran smoothly.

I got a call from Anderson a week later and we arranged to meet them in a barn somewhere in the country. I reckoned it was the place we were held prisoner because when we walked inside it had the same smell. There were around 35 geezers standing around inside the barn and a wooden table in front of them was crammed with firearms.

I told Anderson that we didn't want any heavy weapons on the warehouse sites or at the safe houses. He said the security arrangements were made by him, under advice supplied by us. He introduced us to the SAS-style unit and told us we had nothing to worry about because, as a productive crew, they were unstoppable. It was agreed we'd take care of organising the gigs and leave the rest up to them. They promised that none of the punters would ever get smacked and, if a situation developed, it would be dealt with quickly, quietly and with no violence. We had no choice but to believe him.

GENESIS 1989: FROM STRENGTH TO STRENGTH

Next, we found a venue for 8,000 enthusiasts in a huge warehouse set on a quiet industrial estate in north London. The electricity wasn't working and our sparky couldn't fix it, so he wired extension leads to a couple of street lamps. This winter evening promised to attract by far our largest audience yet.

Genesis, Sunrise and Energy were the biggest dance-party organisations in the country, and one of the perks for retaining such a reputation was the fact that we were on every party, club and pop-concert guest list in London. We'd also have a trail of women from the club entrance to the bar. As I've said before, most of the women didn't mind being used and abused just to be in the company of well-known promoters. They would keep us entertained for days after the event, acting out our schoolboy fantasies. We'd book suites in the Savoy Hotel and have our own private sessions. It could easily cost us ten to fifteen grand a time but, fuck it – easy come, easy go! As Robin Williams said, cocaine is God's way of telling you you're earning too much money.

But we weren't just addicted to the drugs. It was the excitement of the parties, the transformation of a nation, the culture of change. The clothes, fast motors, top restaurants, five-star hotels and beautiful women were pretty cool, too. Your bank account would get severely zapped in the shortest amount of time: on Monday you'd be holding 50 jib, on the Friday you were already squandering the rainy-day stash. My mum nearly passed out when she found out the ridiculous money the suits I was wearing cost. After that, I kept it to myself.

Genesis really was going from strength to strength now, and for this next party we were all fired up and ready to go. The venue looked wicked, and just seeing the warehouse kept me going through all the bollocks we got from the security. Nevertheless, I had a gut feeling that this would be a difficult one and all the blagging ability in the world wouldn't be enough for us tonight. So I got on the phone to the back-up crew and instructed them to set up the emergency warehouse as quick as possible. And my instincts proved right: as soon as I sent somebody down to the meeting point, he was besieged by punters and Old Bill.

'Heads up, everyone, we've got a slight problem at the meeting point,' said a voice over the radio. 'The police are arresting the point staff. Shall we stop them? Over.'

'How many people are down there?' I asked.

'Roughly a thousand. The roads have been blocked off at both ends. We're trapped in between a hundred or so riot police and they've already nicked the lads holding the maps. Over.'

'We've got to somehow get directions to the people outside the blockade,' I said. 'Try to recruit some workers to tell everyone where we are. Start sending them straight away. If you need more help, I'll send someone up to you.'

I telephoned the back-up team to see how they were getting on. Everything was running to plan and would be ready in an hour. I told them that if they were quicker I'd double their wages. When I went outside to check for signs of life, blue flashing lights were tearing down the road and I ducked behind some bushes in time for them to drive straight past. They were looking for the warehouse but our vehicles were all parked inside the building specifically in case this happened.

A load of cars slowed down directly outside the venue and I peeped out from behind the bush. A fleet of riot vans screeched to a halt and I told everyone over the radio they were on to us. I had a few grams of charlie, some puff, the moody lease, a phone and a walkie-talkie in my pockets. If I moved I would be spotted and I knew that attempting a blag could only get me nicked, so I stayed put.

The police ran straight into the warehouse, where there were only 40 staff members. I jumped over a wall behind me and came around the outside of the fence to the main gate. More and more Old Bill vans were pulling up and the police were moving people on. I told a few people the details of the back-up warehouse and the word spread like wildfire. Cars screeched off on their way to the other place.

Keith, KP and some of the crew came casually strolling out through the main gates. They told me Dibble weren't confiscating the equipment, just making everyone pack their stuff away. We sent someone inside to get our cars, and told as many people as possible to follow us. Then we drove in convoy though the streets of east London to the substitute warehouse, a square building on two levels which could hold roughly a thousand on each floor. The electricity source was in working order, and there was no sign of Dibble.

I was feeling very irritable. Our last event had been the biggest warehouse party to date, and here we were now in a building that wouldn't contain a third of the people we expected. Not only were we letting ourselves down, we were waving goodbye to at least 70 grand. But the fact was that these enthusiasts needed somewhere to go, so we had to do our best to supply another building. There were a number of parties that night, including Sunrise, which was somewhere out of London. If our party wasn't a success, that was where we'd be heading.

I telephoned the back-up lads to open the gates and drove straight into the yard. Some of the security were already in place, and 500 party people were standing in line by the entrance. We got inside, quickly letting everyone in. So far, no Old Bill. The venue looked quite good considering the short amount of time that had been put into decorating it. The boys had done a fine job and would be rewarded for their efforts. Sergeant Anderson brought all the equipment from the command centre, and while we waited for the drink vans to arrive, I sent someone to 7–11 to purchase every non-alcoholic beverage in the gaff.

My mood was picking up. The people who had made it this far were really excited about being there. The thrill of the chase had given them an extra rush: they'd been caught in roadblocks, stopped, searched and had to drive across London in convoy, and at the end of it they were standing in a warehouse dancing their tits off surrounded by thousands of people feeling exactly the same way. Nobody cared how big the venue was and the sole intention was to enjoy ourselves to the max.

I was staring out of the small office window upstairs when I saw a convoy of riot police vans slowing to a halt 500 yards from the venue. 300 people were in the yard severely going for gold so I went outside, jumped on top of my car and shouted for everyone's attention. I told the party people that the police were outside and the only way we could win was to make as much noise as possible so they'd think twice about walking through the gates.

Everybody climbed on top of their cars and started chanting: 'Aceeed, Aceeed, Aceeed!' Man, what a feeling! The shouts echoed into the night sky and hundreds of voices sounded like thousands. The DJ inside must have heard us, because the music was turned down and the whole warehouse joined in. A policeman's head peered over the closed gate, then he jumped over and unlocked the iron bolts that held them together. They swung open and a full riot squad stood on the other side. Shocked by the sight, we quietened down for a moment.

The police started making some kind of war cry, banging their shields with their truncheons. They began to move slowly towards us and the people nearest to them ran back to where we were standing. Loads of people came out of the warehouse into the yard. The police cries were getting louder. Shouts of 'Stand firm!' went around the gathering and the chanting started again: 'Aceeed, Aceeed, Aceeed, Aceeed!'

The police abruptly stopped their advance and we got louder and began clapping and jumping up and down. The sea of blue and plastic shields retreated and headed back to their vehicles. The people had won their right to party. This called for a celebration and all the drinks were on us. The crowd were wildly ecstatic and all the grief that had happened earlier that night was quickly forgotten.

I was called to the door on the radio to find Tony and his full crew. The Sunrise gig had been stopped by the Old Bill. I was glad to see them, but sad that their party had been fucked over. At the end of the day, though, this was the chance we took, and there was never any guarantee your party wouldn't be stopped. Unless the venue had a music-and-dance licence, it wasn't legal.

We went upstairs with Tony and two of his people, Alfie and Charlie, and spent the next couple of hours abusing an unlimited personal supply of Peruvian flake. There was a club called the Tunnel Club, ten minutes down the A2, and the riot squad had bravely gone on to raid that.

PART TWO

Hard Times

WESTWAY BLUES

We were feeling unbeatable at this stage in our party-organising career – but this was about to change. We had always known that we couldn't stay one step ahead of the police for ever, and as Dibble grew wise to our plans and began to second-guess our moves, it became harder and harder to organise illegal dance parties. It sometimes seemed that no matter what we tried to do, the Old Bill were wise to us before we even got moving. As 1989 progressed, the happy days of getting away with it were well and truly over and our hard times began.

One example was a party we tried to put on in the spring of '89. Henzil and Lennie Dee were the promoters behind Unit 4, a south-London-based company that produced a series of memorable events with attendances of 3,000 or more. The atmosphere at their events was electric and everyone was out to enjoy themselves. Henzil called me one day and asked us to meet the partners at a venue they had discovered beneath the Westway, near Paddington station. The huge, round building was directly under a flyover and could easily hold 15,000 people. It was the best venue I had seen. There were giant colour murals on the walls, painted for a party that had been held by Mutoid Wasteground, who later became the Mutoid Waste Company. We used to decorate our venues as twilight states, but these guys were a different class.

The Mutoids built huge, moving, fire-breathing robots and sculptures out of scrap iron, and also painted these amazing artworks. The music policy was hard House and Techno – they had a big following who knew exactly what to expect. The murals went around the whole venue and included images of smiley faces, the sun rising, a country at war, a cemetery, the earth and star constellations. The full-colour backdrops looked like masterpieces of modern art. The ceiling was 60 feet up and broken windows surrounded a centrepiece in the roof. There was loads of bird shit, glass and rubble on the deck.

I telephoned a fellow promoter called Jarvis and got him on board, then sent a flyer to the printer. On the day of the gig we went to the venue at midday. It was well concealed beneath the flyover and away from other buildings. It was really easy to find and had parking space for 10,000 motors or more. We brought a team of twenty to help clean the shit up. To make sure none of the glass would fall down off the roof because of vibrations from the music, we climbed up on to the roof and smashed out the already broken windows. It took four hours to get rid of the glass from the panels, but we finally did it.

But all our efforts were in vain. Six hours later the equipment crews turned up outside with the rigs and, as if on cue, a police vehicle came around the corner and pulled up next to their vans. We were peeping through a gap in the wall. Within ten minutes, more vans turned up and nicked our crews. They didn't even glance in our direction.

We got on the phones, trying to sort out another crew. It was 8.30 p.m. and we were running out of time and luck. There was no sign of a system. The generators had been taken along with the vans so darkness soon engulfed the dome. People were turning up at the meeting point five minutes away.

Someone got hold of a lighting and sound crew who were soon en route to the venue. We gathered firewood and anything flammable to light a series of bonfires all round the dome. The murals looked really effective, and flickered in the glow of the flames. We tried our best to hold the fort until the vans turned up.

But the police got there first and quickly put an end to the charade.

GENESIS 1989: THE PROMISED LAND

We were at the peak of our success, where each of our events attracted over 8,000 people, but we knew we had a fight on our hands with the police now, and events from here on in only confirmed this fear. The press and police authorities were now latching on bigtime to what was actually taking place.

The only other promoter staging large-scale dance parties was Sunrise, who had created a sister company called Back to the Future. From their beginnings as a covert operation, Sunrise had raised the stakes and gone overground, introducing membership clubs and using huge licensed venues. They also compiled a national mailing list of people who attended their events. This way they could get word directly to the people that counted, not just at nightclubs and parties but in the comfort of their own homes.

Although Genesis, Sunrise and Energy controlled the monopoly of larger-scale events, a number of promoters staged smaller, more intimate gatherings. You'd see the same set of people at all the underground gigs staged by Kaleidoscope, the Fridge, Shoom, RIP, Hypnosis, Clink Street, Labyrinth, Confusion, Slaughter House, The Hacienda and Queens, a pub in Slough where promoters would meet after parties. These parties were held in London, the Home Counties and Manchester in small sweat-boxes that were home to serious hardcore party animals.

Sunrise initially created the big party boom, closely followed by us, Energy and Biology. Everyone thought that as promoters we earned a lot more money than we did, so you'd meet false people on a daily basis. Gold-diggers were under the impression we raked in £250,000 a gig. After six events they were calling us millionaires. Everyone wanted to know you and hang out with you. A steady flow of bods would walk up, shake your hand and comment about how much you were worth. Even some celebrities said we had more money than them, but I'd have swapped bank accounts with any of them.

Everyone eagerly awaited our next event, from Sloanes and pop stars to squatters from Brixton. An estate agent sold us the keys to a massive warehouse in north London and told us that the building was about to be relet. We did the rounds of the clubs, giving VIP cards to key people and taking names for the guest list. Once you had the faces coming, everyone else followed.

Sunrise were planning a party in an equestrian centre just outside London on the same night as ours. As I've said, there was never any rivalry between our companies. Tony and the crew were our pals and I was glad to see them kicking ass. Tony called to wish us good luck and gave us the directions to the equestrian centre they were using for Back to the Future. His event was legal and unlikely to be stopped. If anything went wrong, I'd be heading straight down there.

We arrived at the warehouse around midday to clean the place up and prepare for the crews coming later. The venue was fantastic, with space for up to 10,000. There were offices at the far end, which backed directly on to our proposed dance floor. They would hold a couple of hundred people and we decided to use them as a VIP area. We created these sanctuaries for our friends, other promoters, DJs and celebrities. Without a VIP area, most of your buddies would get lost in the crowd and might not bump into each other all night. The sanctuary meant that our friends and the faces behind illegal parties could settle down in spacious comfort, skin up, chill out, chop up, get on one or pass out.

Wooden shipping crates littered the building. We cracked open one of the heavy crates and, to our astonishment, it contained a brand-new Honda 550cc. The king of beasts had a logbook attached to its handlebars. There was a stampede to open the other crates and each surprisingly produced something different and very expensive. Designer glass tables, leather sofas, large oil paintings, wooden tables, lanterns, ski equipment, rowing machines, exercise bikes and Persian rugs.

Of course the boys wanted to load them up and ship them out straight away. But I didn't want to chance the owner showing up at the party to discover we'd chored his gear and crashed his warehouse. You had to think of every possible scenario and give even more thought to the solutions. In my book, being able to show the owner his stuff was still there had to be a plus, and a good starting point for further negotiations. If he was prepared to do a deal, I'd offer five grand payment in advance for one night. Waving the money under his nose, while promising to leave the building as we found it, was a sure enough way of capturing his full attention. Then the owner need only tell the officers we had his permission to be there and the law wouldn't be able to touch us or the owner – until the law changed.

We nicked a forklift truck from the yard next door and stacked the crates at the far end of the building. The VIP area was decked out with the furniture we uncovered and the rooms looked better than some houses I've visited. We still had a few hours to spare before the crews turned up. Inspired by the World Cup, we started a five-a-side football match. We started to work on our dribbling skills and attacked each other's defences in pursuit of that winning goal. But the game was interrupted by the sight of two eerie figures, a uniformed policeman and someone in a business suit, walking towards us.

'Are you aware you're trespassing?' asked the suit.

'I'm sorry, who exactly are you?' said KP.

'I'm the owner, this is my building and you are trespassing,' he said.

'I'm afraid there must be some kind of mistake: my father is in the process of leasing this property, and he asked my friends and me to help tidy the place up for him,' said KP.

'Ah! You must be Mr Munroe's son,' he said.

'Yes, that's right. Do you know my father?'

'Oh no, I don't know him personally. The letting agents handle all the paperwork. They've been keeping me up to date with the contract's progress.'

'Are you happy with this arrangement, Mr Barrett?' asked the policeman.

'Oh yes, it's no problem at all. The alarm system automatically checks at police control every three hours. When the signal didn't register at the usual time, the police got in touch with me and here we are. Everything seems to be in order, we won't take up any more of your time. Good day to you,' he said.

'Have a good game, lads,' said the policeman.

'But what about the alarm system?' said KP. 'I'm not sure how it works. Would you mind showing me how to turn it off until we're ready to leave?'

'Follow me and I'll show you what to do. You can keep hold of my key for now.'

The owner switched off the system and explained how it worked. They left the same way they entered. A lucky blag pulled from nowhere!

The first test was over, but our biggest obstacle would be dealing with the police later that evening. After the last event, I didn't feel comfortable fronting the Old Bill on this occasion. My description and artist's impression must have topped the police hit list and it wasn't worth letting my presence jeopardise the event. It was about time everyone realised just how important my role as a negotiator was. If the blag wasn't right and the police didn't think you were a professional, you'd get closed down.

The sound and lighting crews couldn't find the building so I agreed to meet them at a burger stand two minutes' drive away. I ordered a coffee and waited for the vans to arrive. My personal phone was constantly ringing. After ten minutes, three vans came along the quiet road and I waved them down and directed them to the venue.

Everything was running smoothly. The lights, sound and special effects would be up and running by 9 p.m. It had to be done that late as we couldn't take the chance of being discovered too soon. Things had been getting a bit warm for us lately: the police had been asking people questions about the secret locations and our true identities.

We turned the phones on at 8.30 p.m. and they rang immediately. Someone at the meeting point said thousands of people were already there. I gave her the address and told her to bring as many people as possible. I put the group on the guest list and sent someone down to the point before it got out of hand. Minutes later, loads of cars came down the road and I sent someone outside to let them know where we were. The state-of-the-art dance arena was ready. I received a message telling me the police were outside.

I left security to deal with it. There was only 40 people inside so if the blag didn't work we were fucked. My name was being called on the walkie-talkie, but there was no way I was going outside. One of the security came looking for me and told me the chief was giving them a hard time but could be persuaded, if I dealt with it. The police had blocked all roads around the building and blocked everyone in at the meeting points. They were also stopping people from coming inside the yard's perimeter gates. I went outside to the chief.

'Are you the organiser?'

'Yes, what's the problem?'

'You're under arrest. Come with me,' said the chief, grabbing my arm.

'You can't arrest me. What are the charges? This is a perfectly legitimate event,' I said.

I showed him the lease, which he snatched out of my hand without looking at it. Then he handcuffed me and took me to a marked police car. The security all surrounded him, saying that he'd made a mistake: if he wanted the party stopped I was the only person who had the power to do it.

'It's true what they're telling you. I'm the only person who can stop this event. If you'll kindly remove the handcuffs, I'll stop it right away,' I said.

'If you're messing me around, I'll arrest everyone in this building. You're in deep trouble, and still legally under arrest. Now get in there and stop that music. Tell everyone to pack their equipment and leave immediately. When you've done that, return here to me. I think we need to have a long talk,' said the chief, taking off the cuffs and pushing me towards the gates.

I went back inside and the people there gathered round to find out what was going on. I told them the situation and most of them were fuming, saying, 'Fuck the Old Bill, let's stand firm and confront the bastards.' They were tired of being stopped, searched, harassed and deprived of something that meant so much to them. We wanted the party to continue more than anything else. The roads outside were crammed with people on foot. I knew that, if we encouraged the punters, there would be a massive tear-up. The party-revellers were pissed off and if we came out fighting they'd back us up.

But this was against everything Acid House was about. They wanted to battle it out and show the police the people wouldn't stand for it any longer. I wasn't having any of it, especially at one of our events. I wanted the parties to be remembered for what they stood for, not as the warehouse parties that erupted with thousands of angry people against the police. This new generation wasn't about resorting to violence. That was a thing of the past. Our objective was to love our comrades.

I decided to end the party. I thanked them for their support, but the game was up. I changed clothes with a friend and asked a group of girls if they could help smuggle us out of the building and into their car that was parked in the yard. We jumped into the vehicle with the three girls, who drove us out of the gates and past the blockades. We gave them VIP cards for our next event.

There were thousands of people walking towards the venue: it was like a carnival. Gutted and disheartened, we waved goodbye to a chunk of money, turned off our phones, picked up one of the other motors and drove to Sunrise. Tonight, more than any night, I was going to get off my nut and have a wicked time. We put so much energy into organising and promoting the gigs that, when it came to an end like this, the energy was zapped out of you. I could have gone home and crashed out for a week but, fuck it, the best therapy was going Back to the Future.

I took two Calis for maximum headfuck. I used to cane drugs at my own parties, but had learnt to hold the buzz down. Internally, I'd be on another planet but, verbally and physically, I'd be coherent (well, I like to think I was). The mere thought of dealing with police chiefs kept the rushes mildly at bay. I've negotiated with officers after taking a Cali and sniffing a load of toot. Don't ask me how I did it because I surprised myself at times. I think it could be compared to method acting: no matter how off it I became, when the police arrived I'd slip fluently into the character I was portraying. When I spoke to the officers I really felt as if I was that person and, believe me, I didn't take any shit from them.

The chiefs took an instant dislike to us because we were giving it charlie big potatoes. We were young, not bad looking, earning more money than the whole police squad and totally arrogant with it. We were their worst kind of nightmare: rich brats who knew the law and, so we said, had the power of the world's biggest recording companies behind us. Even so, you had to be careful verbally. The trick was not to let your internal buzz get too carried away with itself and to say just enough for them to decide you weren't some moody, backstreet firm but that the event was a meticulously organised music-business extravaganza, with some of the industry's most powerful people in attendance.

The chief I'd met tonight hadn't had any intention of letting the gig take place, he didn't even hear what I had to say. They were here to stop it, whether it was legal or not. I was lucky to walk away from that one. If I'd been nicked they'd have thrown the book at me. Things were getting really hot and we'd have to tread very carefully from here on.

We hit the motorway, singing to Robert Owens' 'I'll Be Your Friend', buzzing from the Calis. There was loads of traffic on the road and it brought a smile to my face to see the heads bopping in the cars going past. Thousands of vehicles were en route to Back to the Future. I really needed this uplifting rush. Cars pulled up alongside us, the occupants hanging out of the windows screaming 'Aceeed!' I opened the window and was shouting back at them. A few other cars joined our mini-convoy. We were driving at 70 miles an hour, yelling 'Aceeed!', and when we weren't shouting our arms would be punching the air to the music. Before long we led a convoy of a hundred cars. Everyone was happy and there was not a miserable face in sight.

The girls who had smuggled us out of the warehouse were in one of the many cars and so were loads of other people who went to Genesis. I told them to follow us and we'd get them in free, which was the least we could do. Thousands of cars were parked for miles around the centre. Luckily they had a private car park for staff and the equipment vans. One of Tony's security was standing guard. He let us park there and I didn't fancy trying to park anywhere else – it was chock-a-block. We waited for the people who followed us to turn up, and then jumped the queue straight to the front. 'Oi Oi.': the whole reception went mad. Tony, Denzil, Charlie and Alfie were jumping around going for it. We told them what had happened before moving inside and Tony let all our guests in free.

Everyone was really excited and eager to party on. Wow! What a party. Thousands of people danced everywhere. The light show was wicked and a powerful sound system echoed through the building. We walked along a gangway looking for anyone we knew and stumbled on a whole section filled with our mates: Delski, Jack, Chris, Amber, Maggie and loads of others. The MC, Chalky, announced we were there because our party had been unfortunately stopped. The section began chanting 'Genesis, Genesis, Genesis!' and we felt a bit embarrassed because everyone was staring at us. They started clapping and the sound rang around the arena until the whole place joined in the chant. The DJ, Fabio, put 'Strings Of Life' on the deck and the dome went fucking barmy. The whole gaff went for it heart and soul.

I remember thinking then that this movement couldn't be crushed: this was something more than drugs, this was an ideal environment to drive home the message of multicultural unification. If it had taken a mind-altering substance to trigger off this change, so be it. It has been written in many prophecies that the level of consciousness on earth will be at its highest point ever at the turn of the next millennium. What was taking shape was an act of fate. Even though most drugs were designed either to heal or to oppress certain classes, Ecstasy was completely different, provoking awareness, openness and love.

As I said, attitudes had been very negative within most communities in inner London and everyone kept themselves to themselves. But in 1988 there was a massive change and promoters provided an ideal opportunity to project this new-found faith on a mass scale. The Es did originally create the environment for such pleasures, but before long they represented only the tip of an iceberg in a global tide of good karma.

The party was at its peak, I was rushing like a goodun and there was this gorgeous chick dancing in front of me. She had a little black dress on, long tanned legs and a dreamlike figure. When you were at parties rushing off your nut, you weren't really thinking about sex: you saved that for when you got home or to a hotel. Parties were about dancing with anyone and everyone. But she was dancing really provocatively, staring into my eyes. After ten minutes I moved in closer to her and we started moving from side to side. I put my hand on her beautifully curved breast; she suffered it and kissed me. I asked her if she wanted to go for a walk; she smiled and followed my lead.

We went over to a corner of the building, still in the arena but set back a little bit. Bales of hay stacked up about ten feet high made a great platform and we climbed on top of the hay and went at it. After a while, we returned to where our friends were originally standing, I gave her my number and she walked off. We didn't even know each other's name.

The rest of the night was brilliant. I hadn't danced like that since Spectrum. I always enjoyed my own parties but most of the time I was really busy doing one thing or another. I hadn't been on the dance floor for more than an hour at any of our events because I had to keep on top of things. That night I danced for seven hours straight and I was soaked right through: I must have lost a few pounds. We all went back to my friend Amber's place in the Docklands and continued the party for another two days.

GANG WARS

I pulled up outside my house early one Sunday morning after being out and on it all night. I was locking my car door when three geezers walked up to me. I recognised one of them as a nutter nicknamed Razor who wasn't all the ticket and was known to stab or cut people at the drop of a hat. He put a big fuck-off knife to my stomach and told me that if I made the wrong move I'd get plunged. A car stopped next to mine and I was instructed to get in. I asked what I had done and where I was being taken. He whacked me on the head with the handle of the blade and then put its razor-sharp edge to my throat.

'Do you know who I am?' he asked.

'I've never seen you in my life. What have I done?'

'My name is Razor and I'll tell you what, mate, I'll fucking kill you.'

'You're gonna kill me anyway, so what difference does it make if I get into your motor?' I said.

'My boss wants a word with you. I won't do anything to you if you get into the car. If you don't, you're gonna wish you were never fucking born. I'm gonna say it one more time. Now get into that fucking car or I'll stab you in the eye.'

I reluctantly climbed in, flanked by the armed guards, and we drove for over an hour before stopping outside a pub. I was ushered into the saloon, where I was confronted by a stocky fella with cropped hair.

'All right, son,' he said. 'You don't know me and my name is unimportant at this time. Let's grab ourselves a table and sit down. I wanna have a chat with ya.'

'But I haven't done anything,' I said.

'It's OK, you ain't got nothing to worry about. Nobody's gonna hurt ya. I'm sorry about Razor, he's like a big kid under all that aggression. How old are you then?'

'Twenty-two.'

'Twenty-two. Fuck me, that takes me back. OK, this is how it is. You're using ex-soldier boys from out of town for your security. Did they force you into using their team?'

'Not at all, a friend of mine from the paratroopers introduced us. They're all right, they do a good job. I've never really thought about where they come from.'

'Well, I'm gonna give you a way out. I want you to call your security team together and tell them to meet you here, within the hour,' he said.

'Have I done something wrong?' I asked.

'Course you ain't. I promise you no one will touch ya. My name is Xuereb, my family is from Malta. Maybe you have heard of me?'

'Yeah, I have, but what is it you want from me or the security?'

'Make all the phone calls you have to and get the whole team down here. You'll know why when you need to know. Get cracking, son, time's running out.'

I rang Anderson and told him what was occurring. I said I'd been taken to this pub and some people wanted to see them. I also pointed out that, if they didn't come, I'd be bang in trouble. It was done. They were on their way. Xuereb was speaking with a group of about twenty geezers who all looked like they could have a right tear-up. Over in the corner of the pub were seven blokes cleaning and loading firearms. I knew our security would be properly tooled up and ready to do battle. They knew this was a potentially threatening situation.

My heart had begun a drum roll that I was finding hard to control. I started breathing deeply and broke into a sweat. This was heavy shit. My mind slipped into survival mode. I glanced around the bar to see if anyone was watching me, then I sprang into action and headed for the door.

A loud voice shouted, 'Oi, don't you fucking move!'

I froze on the spot and turned around. One of the geezers in the corner was pointing an automatic hand-piece directly at me.

'All right, all right, don't shoot, don't shoot,' I said.

'Go and sit down and don't you move again,' he said.

'What the fuck do you think you doing?' said Xuereb. 'What you pointing that at him for? He's only a kid. What the fuck's the matter with you?'

'I'm really sorry,' I said. 'I'm just so scared. You don't realise: if you do anything to them, they could hurt me or my family. They're gonna say I set them up. I can't handle this, I just want to go home.'

'Listen to me and listen good. I'm telling you no one is going to hurt you or your family. I told ya I'm offering you a way out if you want it. All you have to do is say yes. If it's no, you can walk and there's no harm done,' said Xuereb.

'But what do I have to do?'

'When they get here, I'm gonna ask you one simple question,' Xuereb went on. 'Have they threatened you into giving them money? All you have to do is say yes, whether they've threatened you or not. If it's yes, I promise you'll never see 'em again.'

'I can't say that! This lot would kill me if they thought I led them into a trap.'

'Calm down, you haven't led anyone into a trap. They're meant to be your protection. This is what you're paying them for, and you know as well as I do they're not gonna come empty-handed.'

'But why do you want me to say they're extorting money from us?'

'Look, why don't you use your brain? It's only a matter of time before a London firm moves in on ya. If you was clever like I know you are, you'd accept my help. I'm not extorting money from you. I'd give you better protection than those pricks ever could. So fucking what if they're mercenaries, we're not in the bush now.

We're in London. My family name carries a lot of clout in this manor. If you ever had a problem, it wouldn't come to no violence. It's all done over the blower. With the poofs you've got now you'll be constantly tested, no one will let up for a minute. Almost every villain in London is watching what you boys are doing. If there's no name behind you the game will be up. Look, don't worry about a thing. If you want my protection you can have it. If you don't, there's no hard feelings.'

'What's going to happen if I say yes to your proposal? My present security won't just walk away. It's gonna go off severely, and then what happens after you've canned them? They'll be straight round to my gaff, and who knows what might occur?'

'I've already told you nothing will happen to you or your family. Look, I can see you're starting to panic. It's OK, let us take care of it. Don't even think about it, leave it to us.'

'I'm only young, this is all too heavy for me. I'm just an ordinary person. I'll stop doing parties if I can avoid all this.'

'Xuereb, they're here,' said one of the guys standing by the window. 'Where do you want them: outside or in 'ere?'

'Nah, bring 'em in,' said Xuereb.

The huge pub had already been cleared of tables and chairs.

Xuereb took me over to the bar in the middle of the saloon. The doors on both sides opened and in walked Dick, closely followed by the other team members. Everyone in the pub stood up, hands hidden in their jackets, and stared at them.

'What's going on?' said Dick.

'My name's Xuereb and these are my brothers: Keith, Michael, Leyne, Paul, Mickey, Dean and Ian. Being from the country, I doubt you've heard of us. The situation, gentlemen, is as simple as this. Wayne has told me that you and your boys are taking money off him for protection. He said you forced him into giving you money and now he wants to change teams.'

'Well, let's ask Wayne,' said Anderson.

'Don't start giving out your orders here, boy. You think you're the SAS, don't ya?' said Xuereb. 'I'll tell you what, someone get me a pint of milk.'

One of his men passed him a bottle of milk, which he immediately smashed on the floor.

'Have a drink on me, you fucking pussies. Now, Wayne, tell me, are these ponces taking money off you?'

I glanced around the room. Everyone was staring in my direction. The geezers in the corner were holding their shooters, half-hidden behind their legs. The army unit had hands in their coats and behind their backs. My legs started shaking uncontrollably and my body began to twitch. The silence was broken by Xuereb's voice.

'Is that a yes or a no, Wayne?'

I tried to speak but the words wouldn't come out. I couldn't believe I was in this predicament. These guys were all over 35. All I had to do was give them a reason and a full-scale battle would commence. This wasn't like the fights we had when we were younger. The most you'd get out of those was a few stitches and bruises. This lot were actually going to kill each other. It was serious shit. I'd already seen the firepower and they didn't have them for show. My mouth wouldn't budge. Xuereb came over to reassure me, saying I had nothing to worry about and no one was going to hurt me or my family.

'Right, it's over,' he said. 'You soldier boys better piss off and don't ever come back to this pub. One of our lot will give Wayne a lift home, it's not a problem. I'll make sure he's all right.'

'Look, we don't know what's really happening here, but we think it's best we take Wayne with us,' said Anderson.

'Oh yeah? What, don't you trust me or something?' said Xuereb, throwing a pint glass straight at Anderson, which missed and smashed on the pub wall. 'You can fuck right off, before we give it to you anyway.'

'Wayne, call us when you get home, OK?' said Anderson.

'Yeah, I will,' I replied.

The unit walked backward out of the pub and off they went. Xuereb disappeared somewhere in the pub and everyone sat down. Razor, flanked by three others, told me to follow him.

We went outside to the car that had brought me and jumped in. I was sitting in the back with a geezer on either side of me. We drove through an industrial estate, then entered a scrap yard and pulled over. Fear rapidly filled my soul. This didn't look good. Razor was in the front seat. He pulled the Rambo-style knife from out of his jacket.

'You fucked up. You didn't do what they told ya. So now I'm gonna cut ya,' he said.

He hit me on the forehead with the handle of the heavy blade. He was gritting his teeth, holding the blade to my face, while my hands were kept at my sides by the blokes I was sandwiched between. Razor had water in his eyes and was screaming at me that he had to do it. I told him that he didn't because I had done nothing wrong. His phone started ringing and Razor pulled himself together and answered it.

I heard Xuereb's voice shouting at him: ''Ave you took him home yet?'

'Et, nah, I thought you wanted me to give him a smiler,' said Razor.

'What the fuck are you doing? I'll tell you what, mate, if you've hurt him in any way, I'll go fucking mad. Now take him home and get your arse back here pronto.'

They drove me home in total silence. Razor told me to keep my mouth shut or he'd come back. They dropped me at the bottom of my road and sped off. The ordeal had lasted around five hours, and it left me shaken and well and truly stirred. Amazingly, after this mad ordeal, we never heard a word from Xuereb again and Anderson continued running our security, but I was constantly afraid of yet more gangs of psychopaths trying to muscle in.

GENESIS 1989: IN HOUSE WE TRUST

We found a pukka gaff in the East End, set in the middle of an industrial estate. There were landmarks to help the punters' keen sense of direction, and untold parking space. At this stage of our fame we spent more than 25 grand a gig. Considering some promoters spent five jib on their entire campaign and production, this was a chunk of money to lay out for an illegal event. The mission was to create the perfect environment, a surreal fantasy playground and abstract world concealed within the walls of an ordinary-looking warehouse. Our man-made Bermuda Triangles helped transport revellers into another dimension.

We had inspected the gaff earlier in the week, breaking in through an upstairs window for a walkabout to check how much work needed to be done. It was clean as a whistle, the electricity was on and the building was easily secured. On the night of the event, we arrived outside the venue at the usual time, promptly got the trucks inside and went to work. Hours rushed by before everything was almost ready and then I got a call on the walkie-talkie from our man on the roof.

'Two police cars pulling into the estate, heading our way,' he said.

This was a critical time. Gone were the days of going out and fronting it: you'd definitely be nicked if you did that. In the old days, being peaceful and pacifist was cool, but now desperate times meant desperate measures. We were in a corner and had to fight. What we needed was at least 300 people who would stand their ground to the end. It was the only way a party could continue. If you stirred up a crowd to fight for their right to party, the officers would soon retreat and let us get on with it. I decided to turn on the music, lights and smoke machines, to create an illusion of a party already started.

Our man on the roof hadn't been spotted yet. He was watching what the Old Bill were doing and reporting back to me. The warehouse was filling up with smoke and one of the machines was right by the entrance door. We started shouting and making lots of noise and, although there were only twenty of us, it echoed around the building and made us sound like a hundred.

'They're fully kitted up and coming into the warehouse,' said the roof man.

We became louder and more aggressive, calling them all the names under the sun. We couldn't see much, but knew exactly where they were. We weren't really going to have it with them, we only wanted to scare them off, and it worked. They retreated to the street.

'Two SPG [Special Patrol Group] vans are speeding on to the estate, followed by three police cars,' came the word from the roof.

We were the backbone of Genesis and couldn't afford to be nicked – especially me. It was time to leave. We got the team together and told them the koo. The only ones we'd leave in the warehouse were the equipment crews. Dibble wasn't concerned with these people: they were only hired to do a job. We smashed some windows out back and made our escape through the estate, over some trainlines, and settled by a river. The others went their own way, while we stayed within radio range.

The next message we got left us quite shocked. 'Wayne, they're gonna drive a forklift truck through the shutter doors. There's about 30 of them in full riot gear.'

A loud crash echoed into the night. I told the roof man to get out of there. We heard the sound of police radios and saw several torch beams searching the area about 50 yards away. The instinctive thing was to get up and run, but we decided to stay put because they'd easily have caught up with us. Our only escape route was into the river, so we belly-crawled over to the edge and slipped quietly into the freezing cold, rat-infested water. The posse were still moving our way. Shit, shit, shit! The only thing we could do was swim underwater to the other side, or as far away as possible. Even a breaststroke would have made a noise. It was now or never. We faced the other side and ducked under the dark water, pushing ourselves off the bank and coming up roughly ten yards out. The police were already in the area we'd just left.

We had to get out of the water before we caught pneumonia, or even worse. So, submerged once more, we swam until our hands touched the slimy concrete bank. By this time the police had moved on and we scrambled out, freezing our bollocks off. I hadn't realised it was going to be that cold – I would rather have done the bird. We were so unfit I'd say we were in the first stages of hypothermia. Our phones and radios were fucked so we threw them into the water; we didn't want to hide them on the bank in case they were found with our dabs over them.

We ran for ten minutes across marshland to the nearest road. Dripping wet, we ran a gauntlet of streets before finding a minicab office. At first the drivers did their nut, but we told them we'd had a fishing accident and needed to get home before we caught a life-threatening virus. We offered a hundred quid up front to the person who took us. They all jumped at it, and before long we were home drying in front of the fire.

I did catch pneumonia and ended up in hospital for a week; it took me a month to recover fully. On the Saturday morning I got out, we were having a party, so from the hospital I went straight to a warehouse and organised the night ahead.

The crews we'd left in the warehouse told us the demolition men crashed through the barriers with a forklift truck. Everyone was arrested and all the equipment confiscated. Receipts were produced for the equipment and it was collected from police storage. Our roof man made his escape and was home before us. This was a new form of police tactics. The Old Bill in east London were playing for keeps. I don't think they cared who was behind the shutters or in the building. They were determined that somebody was going down.

GENESIS 1989: ONLY LOVE CONQUERS HATE

I first saw a Biology flyer in February 1989. We'd found a warehouse and were out on the night shift with our new flyer, hot from the press. Someone handed me the Biology flyer. The party was billed on the same day as ours, which surprised me. It was a colour flyer with a picture of the *World In Action* logo. They had all the top DJs booked: Paul Oakenfold (whose name was spelt wrong), Norman Jay, Kid Bachelor and a host of other well-known names. It was being held in the Linford Film Studios in south London and they were showing the Tyson v Bruno fight live on giant video screens.

The flyer proclaimed that the function wasn't open to the general public and admission was by invitation only. I got a friend to discreetly acquire some complimentary tickets in case our gig got stopped. I didn't really want to miss the fight and it would be an ideal opportunity to check out the competition and see Bruno get hammered.

We had a loyal clientele so I wasn't really concerned that their gig was on the same Saturday as ours. The more promoters out there organising large-scale events, the bigger and better the scene would become. Our gaff could hold 5,000 people comfortably, and it was in north London, on the opposite side of the road to the huge event (Chapter of Chapters) we'd had a few weeks earlier. The aerodrome-style building was one of several in a row. Only a padlock and chain held its huge doors. Once the chain was snapped, the building was declared open. A warehouse directly next door was still open for business at 7 p.m., so we had to wait until they closed before we moved in and went to work.

Two hours soon passed and we sent a man to the point to direct everyone straight to the venue, which was set back from the main road. It didn't matter how many people stood outside the warehouse, they couldn't be seen. All the main lighting was switched on while the boys added the finishing touches.

There were narrow walkways high on both sides of the arena, connecting one end to the other. I imagine the feeling of walking across was similar to walking the plank of a pirate ship, or crossing a rope bridge 30 feet above a jungle. No room to turn around meant one-way traffic only. At the end of the plank was a tiny square area where we built a tree-house camp as our office. We used a large dustsheet to enclose it, so no one could see us counting the dosh.

People were arriving and forming a queue outside while waiting for the final soundchecks. Then the huge double doors were only opened enough to allow room for just two punters to enter at a time. It started snowing heavily and, though we weren't quite ready, we let the people in anyway. After an hour, the dome was half full, but minutes later a group of SPG vans screeched to a halt and out jumped a riot squad.

Standing by the entrance, I heard the flat-cap say, 'Who's in charge here?'

'I think the organisers are inside,' said a punter.

'Do you know them?' asked the flat-cap.

'No, I saw someone with a management tag earlier,' said the punter.

'Right, I want everyone out of this building in ten minutes. It's time to go home. All you lot in this area, move along. There's nothing happening here tonight,' said the officer.

I grabbed a mate's baseball cap to disguise myself and pushed one of the doors open. Keith opened the other side. 3,000 people stood facing the hundred or so officers. The chief looked shocked, but went on to say we only had eight minutes left. After what had happened at the past few events, I decided it was time for action. I wrapped a scarf around my face and jumped on to the table we were using to take the entry fee. The security circled my position and they were ringed by other punters.

'Listen up, everyone, the police are going to stop this party. It's a legal venue and they're still trying to stop it. It's up to us, we're the only ones that can stop this from happening,' I shouted.

The crowd went mad, screaming, jeering and yelling.

'Oi! You get down from there right now or you're nicked,' said the chief.

I turned to the punters, working them into a frenzy. They started shouting 'Aceeed, Aceeed, Aceeed!' This roar of defiance filled the night air as the police surged forward. I did a swan dive straight on to the arms of the people in front of me, who passed me above their heads until I reached a safe spot where I was let down. The crowd, really enjoying themselves, started clapping. The police held their ground but couldn't be heard over the noise. It was a stand-off: a hundred Dibble on one side; 3,000 party animals on the other.

We all quietened down to total silence and just stared at the riot squad. The snow was tumbling down on their cold, wet uniforms and the chief seemed to be analysing the situation. I think they actually thought that, because we were screaming 'Aceeed!', we must all be tripping. In their eyes, this might pose a potential threat to their safety if they made any attempt to stop the party. We didn't want anyone to start fighting, because eventually we would lose and the entire dance-party movement would also lose.

It was a no-win situation. We knew we'd lose out if a riot ensued, but the police also didn't fancy it – they were on the frontline and heavily outnumbered. They were also freezing their bollocks off! The chief decided to call it a night and let the party continue, and left us to it. Within minutes everything had returned to normal, or at least as normal as our parties ever got.

It was my turn to count the money, so I took a girl with me to keep me company and got up on the walkway, looking over the dance arena, which was jammed with people. She was leaning on the rail, watching the punters go mad, and had a sexy outfit on, which I found hard to resist. I lifted her skirt and began caressing her curves. Anyone who looked up could clearly see what we were doing. I glanced at the crowd below and saw a group of geezers pointing up. She pushed me away, declaring it was her boyfriend who had spotted us. I looked down to see him and his pals heading for the staircase that led up to the walkway. I knew they wouldn't get past my security standing guard. If they did, it meant we needed a new team. She went down to reason with him, saying she had him under the thumb, and I didn't see her again. For the rest of the night, I continued sorting the money out.

Eventually we brought it down the staircase to ground level and one of my mates walked up and told me everyone had been able to see clearly that I was counting money. The candle and torch light made the sheet practically see-through. We cautiously made our way through the crowd. The DJ was shouting 'Genesis '89!' and the hairs on the back of my neck stood up each time he said it. The entrance was fully opened for people to walk freely in and out. When we got out front I noticed some punters arriving with Biology VIP tags on their jackets. They told me the gig was completely packed and, apart from a few disturbances because the fight wasn't screened, it was a great night. But I must hold my hands up and say I was glad it didn't go exactly as planned. Cheeky gits, doing a party on the same night as ours!

We told the security to wait at the venue while we went to the safe house to split the money and return with their cut. When we got there, we shared out the wonga and chopped out some trench lines. Within ten minutes all these cars were pulling up outside the house. The entire security team came banging the door down. They said that because we took a while they thought we might be in trouble.

After they had been invited in and given their share of the profits, the team went home, leaving us to snort ourselves to sleep. Overall, the party was pukka. It was a smaller venue than the one across the road, but at least we were still consistent: the only dance-party organisation to stage a big event week in, week out. If one of our parties was stopped people weren't too disheartened, they knew we'd have another one next week or the week after that. Hundreds of people would call our business lines every day to check whether it was all go the following weekend.

SECURITY TAKEOVER

The fact that we headed the hit list maintained by the police Pay Party Unit meant that most of our gigs were being stopped by now. We faced full riot squads backed by every available officer for miles around. Police intelligence grew stronger and more accurate. With all the police appeals to the public to 'shop a promoter' on their hotlines, outsiders might have viewed the whole warehouse party concept as sinister. The reality was completely different. The aggression was just a front to scare the law away. Nevertheless, we and other innocent people were treated as terrorists or big-time gangsters.

All it took was one phone call to fuck us up. It became a profitable business to plan an event on the same night as ours. On the scheduled night, promoters would keep their fingers crossed and hope we'd get shut down. It usually happened within the first few hours of us setting foot on warehouse property. The police had spies and grasses everywhere. Promoters became national public enemy number one, and a vast network of no-lifers helped to crack the tightly knit dance-party organisations.

I received a visit from someone I knew years ago, now part of a well-known London firm, who told me his associates wanted to meet us. He had also been told to tell me that, if we didn't come to the meet, both Keith and I would have our throats cut. The meeting place was a derelict warehouse on an industrial estate, and I knew it would be yet more nutters trying to muscle in on our security. Luckily, we knew someone who knew another fella who had been around the circuit for many years and was on a first-name basis with all the faces.

He came to the warehouse with us. The door was open so we walked straight in. There were about twenty geezers standing in an open space, dressed in jeans, leather jackets, army greens and tracksuits. Several sports bags lay on the floor. This was getting a bit much – it seemed as if everyone wanted a piece of the action. If we hadn't turned up at the meet, they'd have come and caused havoc at our parties. This was the best way of dealing with it, away and out of sight from the punters. The firm immediately recognised our minder and the mood changed from aggressive to passive. He told them we worked for him and that he paid all the bills. They were unhappy about it but they had to accept his word.

Later that night, I told Anderson and the rest of our security what had happened and where the firm was from. However, the truth was that our security team were beginning to lose interest by now, because every week seemed to end on the same note. The rival firm knew we used ex-army boys from out of town and thought we, as Londoners, should give local teams the work. The soldiers of fortune were agitated at the thought of organised firms showing interest in our affairs. A week later my minder told me that one of the top firms wanted to meet with us and the security. The meet was in the same warehouse as our first encounter. 25 security members came with us, carrying all kinds of concealed weapons.

I didn't even want to go, but I knew our minder wouldn't walk us into a potentially threatening environment. Even so, you don't get much higher than the level these boys were on. If we didn't show up, they'd come looking for us, and that would be a lot worse. We entered the cold, dimly lit building. Standing in the main room was a group of roughly 30 geezers. The mood was very tense and everyone was squaring up ready to go to war. I thought it best I said something.

'I know how this looks but we haven't come here for trouble. You told us to bring these guys with us.'

'This is how it is,' said one of the geezers. 'We've got no quarrel with you three.' He pointed to us. 'Our argument is with your bumpkin-wankers brigade.'

On that, everyone pulled their tools out, from iron bars and baseball bats to CS gas, knives and guns.

'No, hold on a second, what is it you want?' I asked.

'If you think we're gonna let these fucking farmers waltz into town and take money out of our pockets, you better think again.

Now you've got two choices, you pricks. You can walk out that door or fucking crawl.'

'Everybody relax,' said Anderson. 'We're all grown-up people. Let's think about what's at stake. In the past seven weeks we haven't earned a penny. We've lost money. If this scenario had happened six months ago, it would have been a different story. But if you want to take your chances with the parties and the lads, we're not gonna argue. We've had enough, it's not worth fighting for. We're gonna back out of the warehouse and out of your lives. The consequences are too high for so little money.'

'You do what you fucking like, mate,' the London head guy said.

'If we ever see you again you know what's gonna happen, do you understand? You bunch of fucking dicks.'

The London firm were all screaming and shouting obscenities as Anderson's team left the warehouse. Soon after that night I was told our mob had left the country on another of their crazy missions. We were back to square one, in urgent need of a strong team. We negotiated a deal with the London firm, who continued to look after us from that day.

On the whole, the security teams played a small role in the arrangement and promotion of our events. Their real purpose was to safeguard the money. But the aggro had caused us untold grief, and I had to admit that at this stage our parties were beginning to get us down spiritually and financially.

We were nearing the end of our five-month run of successful gigs and we didn't really stand a chance of staging a massive event. Dibble was well on top, and it was hard for us to see a way forwards.

GENESIS 1989: THE EMPIRE STRIKES BACK

We discovered a great venue in east London. It was pukka and would hold 10,000 people. We knew it was a gamble, because the police demolition men were at their peak and hardly any parties in London were going ahead. The only way it was going to happen was if you weren't spotted before opening time, or if you had a few hundred bods prepared to stand their ground. However, we set our date.

The venue's ceiling reached 60 feet at the highest point, which meant we could fit in some fairground rides. Because we hadn't organised an event for a while and most of our last run of gigs had been stopped, the only way we could get everyone's confidence back was to go all out and promote the gig through all channels available to achieve maximum exposure. If we attracted a huge crowd from the off, there was less chance of being stopped.

We wanted to rekindle the Genesis vibe and gear everyone up to make certain the party went ahead. It was planned to be our most spectacular event. We printed three different flyers in batches of 5,000. The first flyer had our logo and the title in green, printed on a black backdrop with a flash of lightning slashing across the night sky. In theory it looked the nuts, but the finished product was cacao.

We printed new membership and VIP cards as well as identification tags for staff, DJs, security and ourselves. This way everyone knew who was who, which meant no arguments. If you didn't have a tag, you weren't one of the team. My sisters, Teena and Nichola, laminated the cards one by one. There were 10,000 members, 500 VIPs and loads of other staff tags. We booked everything well in advance and knew exactly what was available to us on the night. The entry tickets were very important: these were your bread and butter. If you printed cheap tickets, they'd be easily forged.

We issued warnings on pirate radio that members should not purchase tickets from unofficial outlets and should always check their ticket for the official watermark. But people were still attempting to print copies, so our printer went a step further by introducing security holograms made exclusively for him. You could print a message on the ticket that was visible only when held under an ultra-violet light. Ours read 'The Struggle Continues'.

We went out on the town with our flying team and hit the clubs with our first batch of flyers. Clubbers were really excited when we gave them out, and couldn't wait for the gig in four weeks' time. A couple of days later I received a phone call from one of our ticket agents; he told me that Biology had a gig planned for the same night as ours. We thought they must be doing it on purpose to dig us out. The security wanted to pay them a visit but, at the end of the day, how can you pull someone up for having a gig on the same night as yours? It's not as if it was around the corner from our venue and there were thousands of people going to parties, so it didn't really matter.

All it meant was that we had to take our promotion campaign to a higher level and put in a lot more hard work. We recorded a 40-second radio commercial, using the theme from *Chariots of Fire* as a backing track. I read the script from the flyer. We got in touch with several pirate radio stations across the capital, who played our commercial every hour, on the hour, every day, for three weeks. The ad was well received and evoked the desired response. Biology also moved up a gear and flooded the market with their flyers. We shared some ticket outlets and agents in central London. We hit the street with our second batch of flyers, which were pastel-coloured and featured our logo between two Roman columns.

Genesis '89
The Empire Strikes Back (Is Definitely On)

A flash in the pan, it's just a craze, it won't last. The tabloid press blasted us as being an evil cult. They tried to ban this style of music from TV and radio stations, they disillusioned the media with lies they read and heard. And so the birth of Acid House music was condemned as being the root of all evil, forcing the fun-loving people of today underground.

With the government and the media on their side, warehouse after warehouse was and still is stopped whether it is legal or not. During these last two years we have seen the arrival of many other styles of music including House, Balearic, New Beat, Garage and other styles of freestyle music. Many of which have been made by young and very talented musicians of all kinds. To you we salute and to the fun-loving people of this generation we promise to you the struggle will continue, and the fight for the right to have a good time and dance all night long.

The other side detailed all the ticket outlets and information lines. The heat was on and the challenge was set: Genesis or Biology. I knew we were confident; I wondered how they were feeling. A week before the event, we had sold 2,000 tickets.

I came out of my house one morning and noticed I was being followed. A blue Rover shadowed my every move. Instead of doing the usual duties, I decided to go out shopping. Two undercover officers walked twenty yards behind me the whole time. In the end I took them to Henry JB's on King's Road. I stayed there all day with a few friends and got pissed and sent a few beers over to the cops' table every now and then. They wouldn't accept the drinks, but I carried on sending them anyway.

They followed me every day that week. Our promotional drive stepped up yet another gear and we got 2,000 small green stickers made with our name and titles. These were plastered on anything in sight. They were well made and I still see one or two here and there today. We released our last series of flyers, which had a picture of a statue of Zeus on the front and the same information as the first. The Old Bill followed me everywhere, which meant my activities were limited, and they were also tailing Keith.

We had to give a team all the flyers and stickers to flood the West End. On the day, a police team of five different cars were on us. We spotted them a mile away because of the way they were driving. I telephoned our equipment crews to instruct them exactly where to go, and I called our back-up crew to alert them to what was occurring.

At around 6 p.m. we received a phone call from one of the lighting riggers, who told me that they had all been detained at the station for questioning by the police. Both the lighting and sound crews were being held, and shortly after that we received word that our back-up crew were also being held. Someone must have told the police what companies we usually used.

I got on the phone and tried to get another crew to accommodate us, even though it was late in the day. I finally tracked down a lighting and sound company, and asked them to meet us outside the venue. Our police shadow had disappeared, so we were free to hit the street. We went straight to the venue to meet the fairground guy with all his equipment. We turned into the deserted industrial street and, as we got closer to the venue, flashing blue lights came into view. Old Bill was outside the warehouse talking to the guy who owned the rides. He didn't know it was an illegal party, and he must have told them why his trucks were parked in this quiet road.

We had to drive by and we felt gutted. Our cool, calm, collected manner instantly turned to panic. We were at a loss for ideas. I telephoned the ticket outlets to find out how sales were going against Biology tickets. Every outlet told the same story: we were outselling their tickets ten to one. That day we sold 2,500 tickets in six hours and the total so far was 4,500. This left us with two options: cancel the event, or try to get a deal with the competition.

At 7 p.m. I called the Biology office and asked to speak to their main man, Jarvis. We didn't have anything to lose so I told him what had just occurred and asked him if he wanted to do a deal. He was interested, so we went to his office in south London. The offices were crammed with people running around answering the phones and carrying out all the other tasks associated with a big party night. In two words, organised chaos.

After a couple of hours we came to an agreement. We would pay him twenty grand to join up with Biology for that one night. It was a colossal amount of money to pay for a gaff, but it was that or nothing. He wouldn't tell us anything about the venue and to maintain secrecy he wouldn't even say whether it was an indoors or outdoors location. The deal was for a joint party using all his equipment and DJs.

He gave us the address, which we biked over to the telephone company to be put online straight away. We turned our phones on and began instructing people where to go. The event was back on, although our spirits were low and we were still recovering from the massive police operation against us. At least we had managed to find another venue. It could have been a lot worse. The phones went berserk before dying down after a few hours, and we decided to make our way to the plot to meet up with the rest of the team.

We left Jarvis at his office and hit the motorway en route to Meopham in Kent. Hundreds of cars were heading for the party. Seeing them brought back a tingle of excitement, adrenaline started to pump around my body and a smile spread from cheek to cheek. We hit a tailback of traffic five minutes from the secret location. We were in a narrow country lane and the cars didn't move an inch for twenty minutes.

It started to pour down with rain and hundreds of people were heading towards the venue on foot. I asked a group of guys coming away from the site what the venue was like. They told me it was outside in a valley, everyone was getting soaked and there was hardly any shelter. This news came as a shocking surprise.

I felt devastated and we couldn't really say anything to Jarvis because he hadn't said if it was indoors or outdoors – a very clever strategy. We did have the raging hump though. At first we thought we'd been well and truly stung, but soon we calmed down. It was a shrewd business move on his part and we would have done exactly the same thing, especially if we knew the other team's tickets were outselling ours by hundreds. I decided to turn my car around and head back home. I was very disheartened by the whole affair. When I reached home I crashed out straight away, feeling deeply sorry for myself and the people dancing in the rain.

Other than what I've been told, to this day I still don't know what the party was like. The following afternoon I received loads of phone calls from friends and family who had gone. They all had mixed feelings about how the event went. The overall view was that if it hadn't rained it would have been a great scenic visual, but the downpour washed out most of the event. The 4,000 people that did stay danced all night. During that week we announced that anyone who still had tickets for that event could bring them to our next do and gain entry free. Out of all the events that did or didn't happen, this is the one that always comes back to haunt me. Whenever someone has told me they've been to one of my gigs, I've always asked which one. If they say it was outdoors, I know they haven't had a very good experience of my organisational skills.

GENESIS 1989: LIVE AND LET LIVE

The title speaks for itself. But this message wasn't directed only at the powers that be. It was also a message to the promoters (unknown to this day) who kept picking up the phone and informing Dibble of party locations. There were enough punters for us all but someone regularly did the dirty.

They'd send a spy to the meet to get the address of the venue and, once this was obtained, a phone call was made. Before you knew it, the riot squad were turning up in force. This week was no exception and the venue was discovered before anyone had even left the meeting point. The officers, gloating as they basked in the glory of stopping the event, would tell you straight: 'Oh by the way, lads, just in case anyone wants to know, we've done a deal with your competitors: they gave you up so they could have a party instead.' This was the sort of thing they used to come out with, after arresting everyone in the building and confiscating the gear.

It was only 9.30 p.m., and thousands of people were at the meeting point. We kept our phones switched on, telling callers the venue had been discovered and that we were trying to find another one. One of the callers told me he knew a legal warehouse, and that the owner would still be on site. We immediately drove down to the three-storey building in Hackney. It was owned by a West Indian chap who hired it out for wedding receptions, christenings and birthday parties.

We were in luck, the owner was still on the premises and happy to hire us the warehouse for that night. Luck also had it that a sound system was already set up for a party scheduled for Sunday. The only drawback was that we had no lighting equipment, and no chance of getting any. One of our pals had some silly disco-type lights and, under the circumstances, they had to do.

Within an hour of losing the other venue and telling callers where the emergency warehouse was, people started arriving. The place could only hold 1,200, tops. At least we had achieved our objective: this smaller, more intimate crowd could actually get to know one another instead of being lost in a sea of dancing bodies. There was no way we'd make the money back we had spent on the whole night, but our incentive was that our loyal supporters would have a great time anyway.

I was fitting some of the dodge lights to the ceiling on the ground floor. They had to be better than nothing – if we didn't have them it would be pitch black. In walked two of my pals, Kenny Ken and Tony, just when I was telling someone to get hold of another DJ because the next one was late, or lost. The boys told me they were bedroom DJs who had untold records at home and asked if I would give them a shot at spinning some tunes. I was unsure at first because they were beginners, but they soon convinced me and off they went. They both played a wicked set and Kenny Ken gained a fast start on the road to becoming a top DJ, remixer and composer.

I hadn't been too well a couple of days prior to this one and was suffering from exhaustion. By 1a.m. I'd hit the sack and passed out for a few days. I had a fever from lack of energy and a mental shutdown. We lost a load of money on that campaign, but what the hell? That, added to the amount we'd already paid out, came to sixty grand, give or take five jib.

GENESIS BIOLOGY: FUTURE POWER PEOPLE NEW YEAR'S EVE 1989

Much had happened since Genesis Sunset presented The Future is Now. Here we stood on the threshold of what we hoped would be a brighter year. The attendances of 1989 still stand as the biggest ever at illegal dance parties. 5,000 flyers went to print, and the script read:

> *Genesis/Biology*
> *presents*
> *Future Power People*
> *New Year's Eve 1989*
> *On New Year's Eve 1988, Genesis Sunset staged*
> *the biggest dance party of its kind in the world.*
> *It marked the beginning of a phenomenon which*
> *has continued to grow from strength to strength.*
> *You, the people, are responsible for this progression*

from Disco to House, Club to Warehouse, Party to Event, Trend to Way of Life. We dedicate this event to you, the Future Power People. There will never be another 1989, but let us look forward to the forthcoming year with our hands on our hearts and a smile on our faces. So for the very last time this year, prepare yourself for a night of sheer enjoyment. Biology and Genesis salute their members and all party people. 'Live The Dream.'

Keep tuned to all pirate stations for meeting points to be announced at 9 p.m. sharp. This event is completely FREE, all you need is your car and a road atlas.

Come and Join The Future

We put adverts on all the pirate stations and generated a big buzz among clubbers. This night of all nights, thousands and thousands of people were on the lookout for a massive dance party to attend. Hundreds of promoters rubbed their hands together as the world indulged in a hedonistic 48-hour burst of party mania. Sunrise planned the biggest of the bunch in a venue off the M25.

Although it was a great year for a number of reasons, most clubbers had fallen victim at some point to dodge promoters or the police force closing down parties. Earlier in the year, Jarvis had found a huge warehouse in

Slough, previously used as Panasonic's HQ. We agreed it was time to give something back to revellers and we had organised a free party in the warehouse. The gaff was so big that, even with the thousands of people who turned up, it still looked pitifully empty. Jarvis had suggested asking everyone to put a pound each in the kitty towards sound, lights and DJs, who still had to get paid. The production may not have been of the highest standard but, sure enough, there were lights and sound – and we were risking our freedom to stage the party. The Old Bill knew exactly who had organised this unlicensed event, sentences for individuals known to be running illegal gatherings had already been established and captured promoters faced financial ruin, confiscation of their assets and a shit'n'shave in prison.

Jarvis made the announcement over the PA and sent collectors into the crowds with buckets. The punters didn't respond too well. Some people were throwing tenners and scores into the pot, but when the buckets were brought back to the stage they only contained two or three hundred quid. Considering 7,000 people came to the party, this amount seemed insulting and really pissed Jarvis off. He immediately steamed out of the building and we followed suit soon after. The last punters left at 8 a.m.

Despite this, we had decided to use the warehouse again and throw another free party for New Year's Eve.

Hiring the equipment was hard work: no one wanted to rent us their stuff for fear of the police confiscating it. We convinced some guys to do the job, but had to promise the earth to gain their confidence. The police told the tabloids that they knew of three major events, which they were determined to stop at all costs. We weren't sure, but we had a good idea that our event was on that list.

South Mimms service station was announced as the meeting point for 9 p.m. Keith, Jarvis and Tarquin (from *Weekend World*) went to the venue while I drove to the meet. They met the sound and lighting crews at the warehouse and started setting the equipment up. The warehouse was quite dark in places and Tarquin fell down a manhole, cracking a rib on his descent. He probably needed hospital treatment, but there were only two and a half hours left until 1990.

Meanwhile, I reached the arranged meet. The service station was very busy. Clubbers were standing around talking, buying supplies and dancing to car stereos. Everyone was really excited so I asked them to gather round and listen.

'Right then, the plan for tonight is quite simple. When this car and lorry park are full of cars, we'll make our way to the venue. You have to keep your eyes on me at all times, I'm the only person who knows where the venue is. I promise you, no matter what happens here tonight this party is definitely on but, to be one hundred per cent sure, we need your full support. You are the future power people, don't let them take away your right to party. When we reach the warehouse, I want you all to do as I do. We'll be there before midnight, so don't worry – tonight is your night.'

Applause rang around the forecourt. The station was getting busier by the minute and within half an hour the car park was full. People kept asking me when it would be time to go, but I wasn't going anywhere until the lorry park was full. I wanted to have as many vehicles in the convoy as possible. Party revellers sat patiently, near to where I was standing. By 10.30 p.m. the service station was rammed with thousands of keen, smiling faces. Then someone told me the police had blocked both the entrance and exit to the station. I jumped on top of my car.

'Listen up, everyone, tonight Genesis and Biology are staging the biggest dance party in the world. For this to happen, we've got to have you behind us all the way. Let's start this year how we mean to finish. There are two rules when we get on the motorway: I want all the cars in two lanes; no one overtakes my car, if you do you can fuck off now. We don't want any accidents, no driving dangerously. When we reach the venue, everyone must park and wait for my orders. Are you ready? It's party time.'

Everyone was clapping and we got into our cars. My speech had whipped them up into a frenzy and I felt like Moses as a sea of motors parted to let me drive through and head the convoy. At the exit, two police cars blocked our escape. I didn't slow down as I approached the marked vehicles; the drivers didn't think I was going to stop and cleared our path.

We sounded our horns as we cruised past them. This got us even more excited: our first encounter had proved successful. My phone had run out of juice so I couldn't call the boys to let them know I was on my way. The lights of at least a thousand vehicles gave me a feeling of true anarchy. We cared little about anything other than making this New Year's party happen, no matter what. The government, press, council and law enforcement agencies had warned promoters that the bigger events organised for tonight were going to be stamped out. The great minds had made their move; now it was time for the people to respond.

I heard sirens approaching as six police cars came down the outside lane and slipped in front of us. This couldn't get much better, I thought: we had a police escort! When it came to our junction the cars tried to stop us from turning off by slowing down to block the exit. It was like a game of chicken: who would lose their bottle first? I wasn't going to be distracted from driving off at this junction and I think they realised this. We got off the motorway, drove through a series of residential streets and finally arrived outside the warehouse. It was surrounded by an interlocked chain of soldiers and policemen with dogs.

Cars parked everywhere they could and 4,000 people spilt out on to the street. The crowd opened up to let me get to the front. On my way through this human tunnel, I gave them my *Braveheart* speech, my Zulu-warrior cry, my best shot. I told them that if we didn't get past the human barrier it wasn't just over for tonight, it was over, full stop.

By the time I reached the front, my improvised speech had kicked in with the crowd's state of mind: they were screaming and shouting as we approached the chain from all angles. As we drew closer to the men, they made a tactical retreat. We ran towards the building where the only way in was through a big loading bay with shutters. I climbed up and into the warehouse. At the far end of the building I could see policemen loading our equipment into the vans. We started screaming and the police dropped everything and made their escape.

Jarvis, Keith and Tarquin couldn't believe we'd turned up just in time. They were jumping up and down, going nutty. The equipment was set up in a matter of minutes, and at midnight 10,000 people screamed, cheered, clapped, jumped and hugged one another at the turn of a new year and a new dawn.

It was an awesome sight: anarchic, though we're not anarchists. We didn't originally intend to break into other people's property and throw huge illegal parties; it's just that it's the sort of spontaneous action that can ignite and create a way of life. But the truth is that the whole dance phenomenon was being oppressed. At first the police seemed quite happy to let these gatherings go ahead. They knew they were dealing with trouble-free, non-violent events. Only substantial peer pressure pushed them to their attempts to strangle the party scene.

Word got to us that the Sunrise gig had been cancelled and their whole crew were en route to us. We announced it over the PA system and the crowd went wild. At 2 a.m., 15,000 people had gathered together and were going radio rental. Dancing on the stage with my younger sisters, Teena and Nichola, by my side, I was really glad they were experiencing this breathtaking sight. Someone kept shouting 'Future power people!' on the mike. The whole crew was in the house and on the stage dancing to Frankie Knuckles' 'Let The Music Use You'.

The hours flew past and, exhausted, I sat down on the stage and somehow fell asleep. I felt someone shaking me and opened my eyes to see two uniformed officers. They asked me if I was OK. I told them I was tired and waiting for a lift home. The officer said I'd better go outside with them, but I sat up and said I was fine. He then said if he caught me sleeping again they'd arrest me! There were still 3,000 people hard at it when I left at 8 a.m.

The police didn't arrest one single person that night. As we left, the officers wished us a happy New Year and said to drive carefully. For the second year running, we had been part of a joint venture to organise the biggest illegal New Year dance party in the world. It was like the old days all over again.

FREEDOM TO PARTY

During Genesis' short but action-packed existence, we'd seen illegal dance parties get firmly established. Now they were a major part of everyday life and not something we were just going to walk away from. They were worth the fight. The draconian new laws aimed against promoters kept the illegal parties underground and meant there was every chance of a full-scale riot if police showed up at the venue.

None of us wanted a war against the government or their foot soldiers. We, more than anyone, knew that the market for dance music and parties could be developed even further if we went legal and distanced ourselves from the dodge promoters who were now running amok among ticket buyers.

When promoters were forced underground, it meant having to deal with unsavoury characters for the protection of your money and your well-being. By 1990, it was getting out of control and we had somehow to legalise the events before someone was seriously hurt, or worse. Out of every ten parties crashed each weekend there would always be one illegal event organised by some dodge promoters out to make a quick buck and ready to do battle with the law. Something needed to be done to turn it back around. The dance nation was disheartened by the rip-off merchants and the threat of violent conflict with the police, which could easily land even the most innocent reveller in court on serious affray charges.

Despite the occasional big event, many started veering back to the nightclub circuit. But the nightclubs closed too early and by 3.30 a.m. there were thousands of people on the streets with nowhere to go. We couldn't allow the new dance generation to simply fade away without trace. Bollocks to that!

The problem was that licensing restrictions made it almost impossible for organisers to obtain all-night entertainment licences. After the New Year's Eve gig, Genesis intended to organise no more parties, which left Sunrise, Energy, Biology and a host of others to battle with the councils and apply for late licences.

Change is what was really needed. We wanted to identify with our own cult, not one handed down from the Sixties or Seventies. We were like children who had reached a point in life where they begin to create and follow their own paths.

Communication and compromise were necessary. Communication is a vital step in the right direction: the government has to keep in touch with the youth of today. If you don't understand, how can you advise or guide? Compromise is a concept devised to open all the options and safeguard the objectives of all parties concerned. Party promoters had always been willing to talk to government and police officials before the media outrage. But, after a frenzy of misleading headlines and stories, government opinion changed and the illegal parties were almost completely stopped. There was an end to the possibility of compromise.

A parliamentary bill completely outlawing illegal events (by 'illegal' I mean gigs without an entertainment licence) and laying down stricter guidelines for licensing dance parties brought the extravaganzas in line with pop concerts or music festivals.

The MP leading the campaign, Graham Bright, commented: 'I have not found anyone who is in any way opposed to what I'm trying to do, such has been the impact of news stories relating to illegal Acid House parties.' Not one MP opposed the bill. Laws were being drawn up on the basis of tabloid reports and the nationwide hysteria they evoked. Yet clubs all over

Europe opened late: in Spain, Holland, France, Italy and even in Scotland clubs opened until 5 a.m. It was time to change direction and campaign for all-night entertainment licences and later club-closing times.

An Association of Dance Party Promoters (ADPPro) was formed by the linchpins of the four biggest registered organisations: Tony Colston-Hayter (Sunrise, Back to the Future), Anton Le Pirate (Energy/World Dance), Jarvis (Biology) and Jeremy (Energy). They were supported by illegal-party promoters, clubbers, pirate radio, recording companies, DJs, magazines, club owners and a host of other companies sympathetic to the cause.

The date was set for a public demonstration, the first of its kind in the world, which would take place in Trafalgar Square on Saturday 27 January, 1990. Manchester was to host a demonstration on the same day, campaigning for the same rights as us. Not a single flyer was printed but word was spread through all the usual outlets used to promote dance parties. Tight legal restrictions meant no music or amplified sound, other than vocals.

We met up at Biology's office and drove down to the square. This was an historic day in the calendar of dance parties and nightclubs. I remembered early 1989, when Tony and I toyed with the idea of organising such a spectacle. Now our wishes had materialised and we were about to grab the attention of the national and world media. The public needed to be convinced these parties weren't just about drugs and to know we weren't the drug-pushing terrorists we were alleged to be. We were young, ordinary people – neither dealers nor gangsters – who wanted an opportunity to present legal dance parties to meet an ever-increasing demand.

We arrived at Trafalgar Square at 1 p.m. Around a thousand people stood in the rain waiting for the opening speeches. We climbed up on to the first level of Nelson's Column, which stood three feet above everyone's heads. The square was gradually beginning to get busy, and by 2 p.m. 8,000 party people filled the area directly in front of the improvised platform. A van equipped with a full sound system was turned away by the police. The speakers, including Tony, Jarvis, Anton, DJs and Freedom to Party campaigners, spent the following hours making unrehearsed speeches, mainly about our right to party and how basic civil rights were being broken on a grand scale.

I was scheduled to make a speech but changed my mind when I saw how many photographers, TV crews and journalists were on site and taking pictures by the bucketload. I didn't want to put my face up front telling the square I ran Genesis, no fucking way. I'd bet half the photographers were Old Bill, snapping all the otherwise unknown faces behind the illegal gatherings. I wasn't even doing parties any more. There was no way I was standing at the front of that stage. I counted at least 40 photographers, five camera crews and twenty-odd journalists.

It was pouring down as 6,000 people waved banners, sang, danced and voiced their opinions. Someone passed a small generator up to the platform, but it was immediately spotted by the police, who moved in to confiscate it. A struggle took place as police and demonstrators wrestled over the generator, until twenty officers came charging in and grabbed it. The crowds booed and jeered as the officers made off with the power. About 30 mobile phones came out and promoters got on the line to track down a replacement.

One was found and delivery to the square promised within half an hour. Meanwhile, one of the demonstrators, an old school-mate of mine, passed his large cassette recorder over the heads of the crowd and up to the platform. We put the microphone to the speakers and thumped out some House music, which lasted about two minutes until the police homed in on the blaster. We stopped the music, passing the recorder back down to the crowd, who returned it to its owner. We were given a stern warmng by the officer in charge, who said the demo would be broken up and the organisers placed under arrest...

The MC, Ozzie Gee, grabbed the microphone and did a rap about the freedom to party. Everyone was in high spirits and really enjoying the day. After the MC did his thing, a human beatbox took the mike and whipped up a live jam. Next up was Debbie Malone, who sang 'Rescue Me', an anthem on the party circuit. Hands were in the air and smiles on the faces of people who would remember the day for the rest of their lives. People were everywhere and standing on anything that would give them a better view. They danced in empty fountains and on top of the lions that guard Nelson's Column. A cheer went up as someone announced the arrival of a van carrying a generator. A group of people jumped from the platform, rushing over to the gennie, closely followed by Old Bill. A commotion around the van followed and eventually the driver had to scarper. At the same time, an MC, Chalky White, was being arrested. No one knew why, but it completely antagonised the whole crowd.

I spotted a posse of about 30 geezers rushing through the crowd to where Chalky was being held. I could see by the expressions on their faces that they were definitely going to start something with the police. I pointed out the firm to Jarvis and we quickly got down from the platform and headed them off before they reached the squad, reasoning with them not to fuck all the work we'd been doing. They calmed down before disappearing into the crowd. We didn't know why our pal was being arrested but we knew we couldn't win a physical battle with the law. The only way we'd win this battle would be in the courts and with the help of the civil-rights organisations. Violence was exactly what the government and police needed to close the chapter on dance parties for good.

The day passed quickly, and the last announcement was that a free party was scheduled for later that night. Everyone was told to stay tuned to pirate radio stations for more information. Jarvis, Tarquin, Keith and I met others to discuss the party. We didn't have a venue so each went his separate way in search of a big fuck-off gaff. Three hours later, we'd found a warehouse and were about to break in when I got a call from Tony. He said a brand-new place, a huge warehouse in Radlett, had been discovered, and we should make our way there to meet Tarquin, who had already gained entry.

The meeting point was announced on air every fifteen minutes. I didn't fancy arriving at the venue too early, in case Old Bill stormed the gaff before anyone turned up. We drove to the service station where a DJ, Face, was holding the fort. Like rush hour at Liverpool Street, the place was packed solid and traffic was at a standstill. We decided to tell the drivers where the venue was and cleared a path for the lead cars to get through. Gavin and I took control of the traffic flow by the exit.

The police sat back and watched as we organised thousands of cars and sent them merrily on their way. But, in the confusion, the lead cars missed the turning and continued round the roundabout to be confronted by a tailback. We gave the next lot of vehicles the right directions but they too became gridlocked outside the service station. I got my cousin Bobby to drive us through the blockade and on to the venue. About 50 cars followed us down a winding country lane, which eventually led back on to the motorway. When we arrived at the warehouse there were roughly a hundred people inside. The sound system, mobile burger van and drinks vans turned up at the same time.

The building was brand-new and had space for untold numbers of people. It was perfect. The crews began setting their equipment up; it was a complete cowboy job and wouldn't take long to organise. A startled Tarquin asked if I had five hundred quid. A pikey who owned the sound system had pulled a shotgun on him and said none of his stuff was being touched unless we handed over some wonga. We each put some dosh in the kitty and gave the traveller his money.

Two hundred people were now in the building patiently awaiting party time. At one end of the building was a row of ten or so windows looking on to the road in front of the warehouse. Peering out, I could see 30 or 40 policemen running towards the building. The alarm went up as we prepared to be raided. The loading shutters and windows were closed and people started banging on them in a plot to scare the riot squad. The policemen had brought their own camera team and were pointing spotlights on the warehouse. They didn't attempt to enter the building, which led us to believe they were going to try to stop people from getting into the party.

Two guys came up to the shutters and started opening them, and then from nowhere two others ran past us and charged into the police outside. One ran back over to the warehouse and grabbed some Coke cans, lobbing them at the front line. The geezers were going mad, screaming and shouting at the cops, but we got them back inside, closing the shutters behind us. I walked down to where the windows were and looked out to see what the police were doing.

I could see a group of 50 people running down the road towards us, so I got everyone to open the windows and tried to get as many bodies into the warehouse before the long arm got to them. When the officers did reach the people who were left outside, we shut the windows. I was told there was a roadblock about a mile up the road, and that thousands of people were on their way. I looked down the dark, straight road and saw, coming out of the shadows, a huge crowd of people. They were walking in the road and on the pavements.

Spotting this large congregation, the police blocked their route to the warehouse. We opened the windows and cheered them as they started running towards the blockade. The riot police held their ground and stopped the charge while everyone in the warehouse made as much noise as they could. Some people broke through the chain and made a dash for open windows. We opened the shutters and loads of people went outside into the yard, encouraging the others to break the deadlock.

When he saw another huge crowd come charging down the road, the chief quickly decided to let everyone through. It would have been only a matter of minutes before they got through anyway. They made it, the party was on. Everyone was really hyped up, expressing their joy at reaching the final destination. The last head count was 8,000, all well and truly 'aving it. We sent the buckets round at 2 a.m. for everyone to stick a quid in the kitty; it was a good crowd who gladly put hands in pockets. The DJ, Face, accompanied by other top DJs, lined up to play atmospheric sets. It was a great night, which ended around 9 a.m.

On the following two mornings I went to the newsagent and bought every newspaper and magazine in the shop. To my shock, just one small article in one of the tabloids said 500 people attended the demo.

Related music magazines covered the demo but there was nothing in the national or regional press. There was no other mention of the day's events. Surprising, considering that 8,000 people assembled in central London on a cold Saturday afternoon. And where else in the world had a demonstration of this nature taken place? That's news in itself. Thousands of dance-music enthusiasts protesting their democratic right to dance all night long in aircraft hangars, country fields and nightclubs. Come on! We're not living in a totalitarian state, are we? This is England nearing the new millennium: surely suppression of this sort is a thing of the past. Fleet Street and others had been publishing shocking 'revelations' about dance parties and promoters for two years, so what had changed? Why didn't they publish a story on this peaceful protest?

Of all the TV camera crews, reporters and photographers who were at Trafalgar Square, none was invited. Our main objective was to pull everyone together, combining the efforts of the driving forces behind dance culture and, more importantly, the people who attended dance parties. Witnessed by the nation's press, we anticipated the demonstration would make the news. The film crews were rolling for the duration of the rally and crews were directly behind us and had clear shots of everyone. No pictures made it to the TV screens. It's a prime example of how much influence the powers that be have over our tiny island.

A second demonstration was arranged for 3 March at Hyde Park. It started at Speakers' Corner. Although 50,000 flyers were printed, by 3 p.m. only a few thousand people had turned up. The huge police presence was only too visible. A convoy of riot vans in full kit were parked 500 yards away. Promoter after promoter stood on top of soapboxes, letting opinions rip. Then, after a couple of hours, the organisers decided to march peacefully along Oxford Street, down to Trafalgar Square and then on to the Home Office by way of Buckingham Palace. Here the procession was met by a full riot squad, who were definitely not keen on letting us approach the palace gates. Not that anyone planned to cause trouble outside the Queen's gaff – but we did feel an urge to bring the plight of young people to the attention of the royal family.

The rally finished outside the Home Office where a couple of hundred people carrying banners chanted 'Freedom to party'. The demo was badly organised, and received even less press than the first. We knew the government wouldn't listen to our pleas for all-night licences and later club-closing times. But it was still a positive step to advance the cause of dance music and its way of life.

Another objective was to attract the attention of as many members of the public as possible. We hoped to shed more light on dance parties and display our feelings about the way government and police treated the ordinary, hard-working people who attended these events. We wanted the public to witness our frustration at not being allowed to move with the times, and how civil rights were brutally ignored each time a riot squad crashed a party.

Admittedly, in 1990 a lot of people were using Ecstasy, but the rush of actually attending a large, all-night extravaganza was greater than the buzz of the drug. You'd see sons and daughters of lords dancing with Cindy's kids from the corner shop, raggas grooving with hippies, football hooligans hugging, stockbrokers boogieing with telephone operators, sons of MPs chatting on the mike, men of war jumping for joy with men of peace, East End boys and West End girls, farmers getting down with A&R people, Rastamen and baldheads, Mancunians and south Londoners bustin' moves, film and pop stars drinking with shelf-stackers and postmen, mums and dads, Sloanes and rappers, page-three girls and car dealers, Poms kissing Sheilas, road sweepers swinging with undercover cops, libertarians philosophising with labourers. The list goes on and on but, whoever attended, gatherings of this kind posed no threat to national security. Partygoers only felt the need to fight back and, if necessary, physically defend their civil rights, after months of being repeatedly intimidated by the heavy-handed tactics of the law-enforcement agencies.

GENESIS 1990 AND FANTASY FM RADIO: THE WAREHOUSE EXPERIENCE

Despite having said we'd had it with parties, we were annoyed at the numbers of rip-offs and dodge events going on. We decided Genesis should make a comeback after we were approached in late 1990 by one of the best pirate radio stations, Fantasy FM.

Foxy was the driving force behind Fantasy and I met him at the Biology office. He and Jarvis had just closed a deal regarding recorded telephone lines. Jarvis hooked up with a service provider who owned every 0839 number that existed and leased both parties (and us) as many lines as were desired. The numbers were constantly plugged on radio, and advertised and printed on hundreds of thousands of flyers, posters and all other promotional literature. He used the exposure to push his newly founded company to businesses and other service providers.

Benn loved everything about the parties. They completely changed and engulfed his life: he was always running around going nuts. He was a true character who I got on well with. Like most workaholics, he was constantly running his mind and body into the ground, without replacing vital vitamins to maintain the pace. This, added to the effects of class As, can only lead one way and that's downhill. The pressure became too much and his father sent him on a world cruise aboard his own motor yacht (that'll do nicely!)

We leased 20 phone lines for Genesis. They had to be updated regularly, so I visited the offices daily. Although the law had declared a ban on the announcement of dance-party locations on recorded telephone lines, there were a number of services that could be provided: event information, mailing-list registration, merchandise and ticket outlet names.

We discovered another huge venue, which could easily hold 10,000 people. It was close to a housing estate, situated in the East End. The police in this part of town had already shown that they didn't want parties, full stop. If the event was to be held here, there'd have to be a strong firm ready to counteract police tactics. I mentioned the plot to Foxy, who suggested a joint venture. I thought it was a good idea, because maximum airplay was guaranteed. Fantasy FM was a very popular station with a large following: a line-up of wicked DJs played live House and hardcore sets, 24 hours a day, seven days a week. We negotiated the terms and the event was set for two weeks from that day. We didn't print flyers. The party would be promoted on the air, and a series of commercials were recorded using my voiceover and broadcast on the hour every hour. The backing track was 'Can You Feel It?' by Fingers Inc. and one of the scripts went like this:

The Summer of Love 1990 has begun.
And so once again we will witness the rebirth of warehouse fever.
In a very large secret location somewhere in London.
We promise you a night filled with excitement, adventure and, above all, somewhere to dance all night long, surrounded by thousands of people with the same intention.
Genesis and FR promotions present The Warehouse Experience.
In the house exclusively for your entertainment will be Coolhand Flex, Kenny Ken, DJ Hype, DJ Flirt, DJ Rap, The Rhythm Doctor, Mickey Finn, plus special guests.
Visuals consist of a full lighting rig, special effects and lots more.
Entry is just five pounds.
All meeting points will be given out on Saturday night. The main convoys will leave the points at 12 sharp.

*Keep tuned to this station for meeting points and
more information as it comes.
Genesis and FR promotions present The
Warehouse Experience. Saturday night – be there.*

After all the let-downs of parties being stopped, we decided to charge a five quid entry fee. We wanted to do it for free but we had to cover costs and it was a small price to pay for such a big event: ticket prices for some gigs were as high as £25. Our names were up front, which meant we could be arrested and charged for promoting the event, so we were taking a major risk. We gave ourselves two weeks to promote it and thrashed the bollocks out of the airplay, with three different commercials playing until the night before the event.

We sent our people to the meeting points and Foxy went to the meet at a club called the Shenola in Hackney. At 9 p.m. when the meets were announced, he was sitting quietly in his motor waiting for the revellers to begin arriving. We sent some workers to the warehouse: it was their job to break in and prepare the venue. At 9.15 I was telephoned by my sound guy, who was held up because some undercover police officers were plotted up by his van outside his house. He tried to throw the police by driving off in the wrong direction but they still followed him. It was too risky for him to take a chance and drive to the gaff, so we decided not to use his equipment.

I got on the phone, trying to sort out another system in time for the 10 p.m. start. I finally tracked down an old reggae sound system and crew and instructed them to meet my boys at the venue. Foxy called me to say there were a couple of thousand party animals at the meet and he was starting to panic. I said he should send some of the people, but not all of them, and I would meet them at the warehouse. When I got there, about 500 people were standing outside in the street. They were talking to a group of policemen and someone told me that one officer had said we should go ahead and have the party.

Right at that moment, one of the sound boys came outside and said he'd left some speaker connections at home. When the officer heard this, he said, 'Right, that's it. There's no party here tonight.' Two riot vans pulled up and a squad of police jumped out. They blocked the way to the venue and stood facing us. Everyone was gearing up to have it with them. A girl tried to break through the police line and was grabbed, punched and hit with truncheons before being chucked into a van. About twenty people ran forward and steamed the Old Bill. The coppers were going mad, hitting anything that moved.

The fighting stopped for a moment and a breakaway group of about 50 people headed off round the back way. They were running down the quiet road towards the building when three vans pulled up in front of and behind them. A small battle took place but no one was arrested. It was as if we were being taught a lesson by way of a good beating. But that was it – the party was stopped. There was no way I was willing to continue trying to get in, even though I knew that if Foxy sent over the rest of the people we might have succeeded. The police were not playing around that night and I didn't want to risk a full-scale riot. We'd suffered yet another heavy defeat.

PART THREE

Pills and Bullshit

DANCE WITH THE DEVIL

Like everybody, I have many bizarre memories of the Acid House days and they're not all bound up in Genesis and organising my own parties. Sometimes me and my mates had the very best times when we were giving it loads at other people's events and freed from the crazy and exhausting pressures of staging the parties and having to look out for Old Bill ourselves.

I quite often went clubbing with a load of mates to an old barn in South Ockendon, Rainham. This was a great little venue that only a few people knew about. The barn had been transformed into an ultraviolet dance arena that held around 500 people. We would always be tripping off our nut, going wild to Acid House music and lost in a sea of smiley-face T-shirts.

One night a load of us went there and one of our mates, Andrew, brought along a friend of his, Paul. The guy had never been to a dance party before, or taken class-A substances, but he had heard about the tricks that Keith and I used to get up to and was advised to stay well away from us.

Amazingly, Andrew gave his own pal his first trip. I told him he must be mad. To give someone a tab and send them into a small UV-lit shed is not a good idea. The fella stood 6 foot 4 inches, so he was a big lump. We were all dancing while he stood there observing what was happening. Within one hour of dropping the strawberry tab, Paul suddenly bolted for the exit. When he reached the security-manned door he started screaming and everyone moved out of the way. Andrew went after him, leaving us lot to get on with it.

A couple of hours passed and we were sweating, so we went outside for some air. We walked over to where our cars were parked and heard muffled screaming. As we got closer to the cars, we noticed someone going mad and trying to get out of our friend's Peugeot. We saw that it was big Paul; he dived on to the ground, got up and glared at us, then said we should go away because we were making his buzz come back. He turned around, hopped over a fence and shot off through a field. Andrew went after him and we went back inside and got on with some serious dancing. We visited the barn four Saturdays on the trot, then one Saturday we turned up to find that the shed had burnt to the ground. So that was the end of that.

THE DUNGEONS 1989

Hypnosis were the original promoters to use this venue back in late 1988 and early 1989. Licensed buildings were a blessing back then and, although this was a dingy, claustrophobic venue, most of the original people who attended Acid parties have been at least once to The Dungeons, situated in Leabridge Road, east London, below a pub formerly used by Hell's Angels.

Promoters used the building midweek, after club nights in the West End. Punters who didn't want to go home whilst still high on the effects of Ecstasy could release their remaining energy here. Linden C and his crew had transformed this maze of arch-shaped tunnels into a great dance space where the sound-and-lighting system blasted you to another planet. The tunnels were covered with UV backdrops and the abstract murals looked 3D when you stared at them, especially if you were buzzing. The Dungeons was packed to the max each week, before finally dying out in the face of competition from mega-sized events.

I was upstairs there one night and some of my mates were completely off it. One of them, Lloyd, had only recently started dropping Es. The pub overlooked a forecourt where tables and chairs made a perfect chill-out area and a place to cool down from the raging furnace of the heat inside.

Without warning, Lloyd suddenly launched himself through an open window. It was only a ten-foot drop, but fuck! He did a butterfly dive towards unsuspecting clubbers down below, and screams rang out as we rushed down the fire escape to check he wasn't seriously injured.

Fortunately, his eleven-stone frame had landed on a table. It had been full of drinks in plastic cups, and fluid was everywhere. Lloyd jumped up immediately, before the security guards (flanked by us) escorted him off the property. Reasoning with the guards didn't deter them from banning him from the gaff indefinitely. Lloyd's only souvenirs of the incident were a lump on the head and a slight case of amnesia.

ENERGY

I first met the Energy promoters outside a warehouse in Hackney on a Saturday night. Along with Linden C, we gained entrance to the huge warehouse, which could have held eight to ten thousand people. The electricity was in full working order so we called in the equipment crews and began setting the gear up.

We were carrying a huge speaker to the upper floor, which held another few thousand, when a middle-aged geezer with a German shepherd dog appeared from nowhere. He didn't say a word as he slipped past us and out of the main door, and we continued work without giving the incident another thought. However, within half an hour a single policeman came walking up the staircase and told us that the police had been called by the owner and we had no right to be on his property. It seemed that firms in the area had started hiring night watchmen to stop anyone from putting on parties. We tried to offer the policeman a bribe to turn a blind eye and even offered to clean up the building when we'd finished but he wasn't having it.

Soon afterwards, the Energy boys joined up with Anton le Pirate, who had designed and created a fantasy film set at the Westway film studios in Shepherds Bush. This was one of the best parties I've ever been to. Each huge dance arena had its own theme. I remember standing in the main room, where a massive Roman temple had been erected as a centrepiece. Lasers bounced around the arena and created an awe-inspiring spectacle. Anton stood on top of the set, dancing and giving it loads. I can imagine how he felt – this party was the bollocks.

The Cali I had dropped earlier was starting to take effect, and the music levels seemed to be growing louder and louder. I felt as if the music was controlling my every move, and spasms shook my body as the rushes went from the tips of my toes to the tips of my fingers. The music seeped into my brain cells and my mind. Submerged in music, I danced to the song of freedom. My hands were in the air, my eyes closed, and my body jerked for joy. When I stopped for a moment, laser beams were piercing the top of the studio as huge strobe lights intensified in the background. I looked around the arena and connected with the energy projected by thousands of people. It seemed as if we were all on exactly the same level.

When a special part of a record came through the mix, everyone responded. The DJ was right there with us every step of the way and took us on a journey through the archives of House music. There were people standing with their arms raised, hypnotised by the lasers overhead, singing, 'This is, This is, This is, This is, This is, This is the real life.' I'll remember that party for many years to come. Fucking awesome!

CLAPHAM COMMON

Another superb event took place on Clapham Common. There had been rumours of a spontaneous party, and we joined the convoy and went in search of space. We reached the Common and found nothing happening. Most cars didn't bother to stop, and just drove off into the sunrise. However, because it was a beautiful morning we decided to chill out for a while on the grass. Before long, a thousand hardcore party animals had converged on the Common and started dancing to car stereos and ghettoblasters.

The following week, some party enthusiasts tried to drive vans equipped with sound systems and speakers on to the green but police were quick to stop and escort vehicles out of the area. During this cat-and-mouse game some clubbers smuggled a smaller system on to the Common, but unfortunately the generator supplying the power was louder than the music. The police returned and found around 200 people huddled around the weak sound source. Somebody started throwing bottles at the law and they just turned around and left us to get on with it.

DANCE '89

On one occasion, Dance '89 organised a huge party in memory of the *Marchioness* disaster on the River Thames. This much-publicised event encountered a number of problems with the police force and the environmental health department. The police discovered where the warehouse was, and completely sealed it off within a security blanket. Nobody could get near the gaff.

An alarm was sent out, and a substitute aircraft hangar was found at sunrise on the morning of the party. The venue details were relayed through the phone lines and a game of hide-and-seek began. It was 7 a.m. when we reached the site and found a 3,000-strong queue of people stretching around the runway in front of the hangar.

None of the original promoters were on site as the staff hurried to get the systems operational. An articulated truck full of speakers ripped into song as the needle hit the first record. Before long, 10,000 people were dancing, clapping and singing in the full glare of the burning sun. Two wooden sheds, one 30 feet high and the other about half the size, made great platforms.

One of my mates, Troy, was giving it some on the highest stage while fifteen others danced on the smaller structure. Its roof looked fit to collapse under the weight, so I made them get down before somebody got hurt. Twenty minutes later, a totally square middle-aged couple approached me and said I had been pointed out as the promoter. They turned out to be the extremely angry owners, who started shouting at me. I said the party had nothing to do with me and walked away from them.

Around five o'clock I left the site and stepped straight into a war zone. Four cars were engulfed in flames and panic-stricken clubbers ran around like headless chickens as other drivers tried to move their cars out of harm's reach. There was no water for miles and, with not a fire engine in sight, cars were left to burn. Black smoke corrupted blue skies. People were dancing around the fires. To the townsfolk it must have resembled devil worship, which would only confirm the lurid claims that were currently being made in the press. Apparently the fire had started with a discarded cigarette on dry grassland.

I left the hangar at around 6.30 p.m., went home and crashed for the night. I'd only just got to sleep when my phone rang and it was KP, who was lost and ringing from a call box somewhere near the party. He'd pulled a bird at the hangar and disappeared, only to return later and find that everyone had gone home.

I couldn't even remember where the party was as we'd found our way by following traffic. I had a vague idea of the location but it would take a while before I found a call box in the middle of nowhere. Armed with the minimum of coordinates, I set out in search of my pal and his chick. An hour after locating the hangar I came across the couple, huddled together like a pair of freezing kids.

ENERGY – DOCKLANDS ARENA

Energy staged two huge events at the Docklands Arena and I went to both of them. The sound-and-lighting production were great, but the gigs lacked Energy's usual vibe. They were more like conventions for Sharons and Trevors who'd come along to discover what all the hype of 1989 was about, and an army of police officers patrolled the arena for dealers and users.

I went to the second Docklands party with my mate Darren and his girlfriend Alice. We had complimentary tickets, so didn't have to stand in the thousand-strong queue to get in. When I saw how many people were outside, I thought it was going to be a good day. Licensing conditions meant they could only run from noon to 8 p.m., which was a real bummer but a good start to legalising such events. I only had a pill and a lump of puff hidden in my Calvin Kleins, and Darren had an eighth of charlie. We got past the reception where about a hundred security men searched people and bags, and entered the arena, which was only a quarter full. I reached into my trousers to retrieve the substances and there was a minor commotion before some geezers in baseball caps came out of nowhere and grabbed hold of us. They were Old Bill.

I was lifted up and carried through a fire exit and along a maze of tunnels. An officer held my arms tightly so that I couldn't reach the stash and drop it on the floor. As they marched me along the officers asked me what I was carrying and I told him I only had a bit of personal puff on me. He said that if that was all I had they would let me go, but if he found anything else I'd be nicked.

We went into a huge room with glass windows that went all the way round it. There were around 60 police officers in the room, some of whom were taking pictures of the crowds, while others were looking through binoculars. We had to empty our pockets before two coppers thoroughly searched us. I was asked to drop my trousers, which I did. The puff and pill fell on to the floor and I was promptly arrested. When Darren dropped his strides his wrap of charlie fell on the deck. I heard an officer ask him what it was and he said it was speed. They handcuffed me and let Darren go.

I was led again through a maze of tunnels that led on to an upper-level landing, looking directly over the dance floor. To my astonishment, hundreds of policemen were sitting around, spying on the unwitting party revellers. The observation team couldn't be spotted from the dance floor. There was me thinking what a positive step this party was, when in reality it was a huge police surveillance operation. The more people they arrested for possession or dealing, the harder it would be to be granted music and dance licences.

When we got to the ground level I was taken through a back door and into a van. There was a group of ten plain-clothes, black, female officers, who were dressed in sexy shorts, high heels, the lot. They had hold of a few geezers who looked well shocked. I was taken to a police station and charged with possession but my friend Darren didn't even get nicked.

I knew the Energy organisers had the right intentions, but they'd made a mistake in even contemplating bringing the police and partygoers together. Not just that, I'd say, judging by the attendance, that they must have lost money after they'd put all those Old Bill on the guest list. That was pretty much the end of the original Energy, which was then taken over by a company in north England who continued to arrange dance parties.

BIOLOGY

Wednesday nights at the Café de Paris were essential for late-Eighties clubbers. It wasn't a T-shirt job: everyone dressed for the occasion. You'd find all the faces from England's entertainment industry in attendance, along with the boys from the hood and others. I met a lot of promoters at these events; meetings would usually begin with sarcastic humour, then either a friendship would develop or the companies would be set on a head-on collision course. But what was the point in promoters being enemies? We were all out to achieve the same objectives. So I agreed to help out Biology with their promotion.

Genesis, Sunrise and Energy had already earned the respect of clubland, and Biology now joined the ranks. We'd planned on having a break from the stressful life of arranging such events – our past eight attempts had been crashed by Old Bill – so we welcomed the opportunity to let our hair down, party hard and let somebody else take the stress. Summer 1989 was a scorcher and saw a series of outdoor gigs. One major one was Biology's DJ Convention, on a site in Watford for 10,000 people.

We needed a hype flyer and came up with the caption 'Why Can't We Dance?', which was simple, effective and to the point. We printed up 10,000 flyers, which were distributed at clubs across London. I also suggested that we should do a radio ad for the event, and volunteered to write a script and have it recorded. Everything we needed, from the sound system to drinks, had already been arranged. The only thing left to do was blanket promote the gig across London, so I went to the Noise Gate Studios and put this radio commercial together:

This is a Party Political Dance Broadcast on behalf of the Biology Party.

Here are the following requirements for this Saturday's DJ Convention and gathering of the young minds:

Firstly, you must have a Great Britain road atlas. Yes, that's a Great Britain road atlas.

Secondly, a reliable motor vehicle with a full tank of gas.

Last, but not least, you must have a ticket and you must be a member.

Your membership cards entitle you to free drinks all night. So we now end this Party Political Dance Broadcast on behalf of the Biology Party. Don't waste your vote: stand up and be counted, because Biology is ON.

It sounded the nuts and we were all very happy with the finished product, which was transmitted on pirate stations across the region.

On the day of the party, the Biology promoter, Jarvis, came for me in a stretch Mercedes. We spent the entire day shopping and drinking on the Kings Road, where the latest designer clobber left us five jib out of pocket.

The day quickly passed and we were soon en route to the venue in Watford. A pub called The Game Bird was one of the meets, just five minutes from the field we were using. We stopped there on our way through; the road for miles around was busy with traffic trying to find the site. The pub landlord couldn't understand what was happening, but we assured him there was nothing to worry about and said we'd send the limo back to bring him and his wife to the party, so they could see the show for themselves.

Biology had sold 4,000 tickets earlier that day, so we knew it was going to be a big night. When we reached the site, the staging, light show and sound system looked and sounded awesome. There were thousands of people there and it resembled a live concert as a collective line-up of DJs thrashed their sets out. There were side stalls along the field's boundaries where everything from drinks to clothes was on sale. The atmosphere was electric and there wasn't a policeman in sight.

The site was hard to secure and people were bunking in where they could. Most party revellers did have tickets, so it wasn't a big problem. I was on the stage looking out at the thousands of bopping heads, reconfirming my belief that this wasn't a phase that was going to quietly fade away. Jarvis brought a van full of champagne for his pals and we all cracked a bottle open and sprayed the crowd. It sounds like an ego trip but it wasn't, we were just happy the event was taking place and felt this was a victory and progression for promoters.

This was the first outdoor dance party of its kind and it had taken a week to build the stage, without so much as a whisper from Dibble. We grabbed the opportunity to dance the night away in the middle of a field. The night was a huge success and Biology had pulled it off. The last guests left the green at 2 p.m. It was a beautiful sunny day and those that weren't dancing were sunbathing.

SUNRISE 1989

Without a doubt, Tony Colston-Hayter and his team at Sunrise/Back to the Future were the most organised dance-party promoters on the circuit. They'd arranged some of the best gigs I've been to, and have to be the most well-known company in England. They were largely responsible for bringing dance parties into the mainstream and the public eye.

Tony appeared on a number of chat shows, including Jonathan Ross's show, where he handcuffed himself to the host as a protest against the new government bill, which had outlawed the events full stop. Jonathan Ross had to be cut free by the studio floor manager, and threatened to punch Tony on the nose. The next day the press reported stories about Tony offering Ross out in a boxing ring.

The press continued publishing headline stories about Sunrise parties and personal articles about Tony, the man they labelled The Acid King. One of his biggest gigs was in an aircraft hangar in White Waltham, which turned out to be the highest-profile event in the history of dance parties. One front page read: 'Spaced

Out: 25,000 Trippers At Britain's Biggest Acid Party'. Another reported: '20,000 People On Acid'.

I couldn't say precisely how many people were in attendance but I did know it was the biggest gig I'd been to. We stopped at a service station en route to the hangar where hundreds of lost people had congregated. Tony had given me directions to the venue, so I got them all to follow me. The convoy included a hundred cars or more. The headlights illuminated the long, dark roads and country lanes. I was driving the lead car, which gave me a clear view of what was up ahead. We were on a narrow lane when I spotted a small convoy of British Army vehicles carrying some kind of war missiles. I would have loved to see the expressions on their faces when they looked into the rear-view mirror and saw a huge convoy of cars coming up behind them, especially on a normally quiet lane with barely a flow of daytime traffic. Why these hundreds of cars in the early hours?

I was right behind the transport carriers, who were driving at 30 mph. When the opportunity came we overtook the trucks and pressed our horns, screaming 'Aceeed!' The soldiers returned the compliment, shouting at the top of their voices. It took about two minutes for the convoy to pass the squaddies, then we moved on to the hangar.

On entering the site we were confronted by one of the largest gathering of dance-music enthusiasts I'd ever set eyes on. The sound system ripped through the hangar and vibrated the ribcages of the people standing next to the speakers. There was a multi-tiered dance platform erected in the middle of the arena, which was packed with people getting down to some House music. It was a moving experience to see and feel the energy and atmosphere of this huge gathering.

At 10 o'clock the next morning the sound system was turned off and the last few thousand revellers were asked to leave the building while the crews recovered their equipment. A fellow named Mark pulled up outside the hangar in a red Ford Sierra, which packed a deafening stereo system. It was a beautiful sunny day, and 200 people danced to his stereo until 6 p.m.

On the way home, we stopped at a service station and were shocked to see the event had made front-page news. Sunrise went on to organise a series of massive parties in different locations around the country, and as we all now know, their much-publicised gigs became a national underground phenomenon.

ESTABLISHMENT REACTIONS

The media had been sniffing round the Acid House scene for a while and after Sunrise's huge event in White Waltham, Fleet Street had a field day. The journalists were hyped up to the max and published misinformed articles, which told how the hacks had risked life and limb to bring their stories to the public's attention. First, they called promoters Mr Big, then topped the assault off by calling us drug barons. They blamed promoters for anything and everything that happened within a 20-mile radius of any party location.

In all honesty, if the press hadn't given the topic as much editorial coverage as they did, dance parties might have died a quiet death and remained underground and attended only by a select few. Then suddenly, in as little as one month, everyone in Britain had heard of Ecstasy and the huge, secret, illegal parties. The stories stirred up interest from people all over the country. I'm not saying it was all down to the press, and it's quite possible the nation would have caught on without the media's focus. But it would have taken a very long time before our nans and granddads would have heard of Ecstasy.

The newspapers brought E to the doorstep of every household in England. The people who did make the drugs couldn't have wished for a better promotional campaign. This was their dream come true. We'd be partying hard at Energy, Sunrise or another big gig, and on the way home we'd stop at a newsagent and buy three or four national newspapers with front-page stories about where we'd just been. The same went for regional, and local, tabloids, as well as magazines, TV and radio stations.

One of the all-time classic examples of a sensationalised story in a national newspaper told how a journalist bravely risked personal injury to take the famous pictures from White Waltham that appeared as part of a huge spread. He said he discovered thousands of Ecstasy wrappers covering the hangar floor, and built a whole story around this theory. Ecstasy wrappers? I have never in all my past years of taking pills seen an Ecstasy wrapper. If anyone out there has seen one, please send it for my attention via the publisher. I would be most interested in examining this unique paraphernalia.

What the reporter actually saw was tiny squares of silver paper, the kind that comes from a theatrical special-effect explosion. As far as risking life and limb goes, they must have been pushing their bosses for danger money. Nobody cared about their picture being taken and the only people that wouldn't have liked to be photographed would have been promoters and their security teams. I have a huge selection of newspaper and magazine cuttings from 1989–90, and in the hundreds of pieces in my collection there are no pictures of promoters, staff, security or DJs at illegal dance parties. If the journalists were threatened, or if their cameras or films had been confiscated, you can be sure they'd have told us all about it.

Even though journalists bombarded the public with bad press, in one week during 1989 five dance recordings stood defiantly at the top of the charts. Acid House's most aggressive opponents were the tabloids, yet Radio One and other stations also banned any record that used the word 'acid' as part of a song. No matter how high the record reached, it was censored or had to be changed on specifications laid down by the radio authorities.

The press invented their own frownie face instead of a smiley symbol, and one national tabloid launched a 'Ban Acid House' campaign and recruited a host of pop stars to speak out against dance culture and Ecstasy. Up until the media attention, you'd see most of these artistes off their nuts dancing in front of a strobe light every Saturday night. It's no surprise that pop stars spoke openly about outlawing the dance parties. Their careers were at risk and, to add insult to injury, their replacements were to be utterly unknown DJs and producers from England, the USA and Italy. Kids were no longer interested in worshipping pop singers: in the Acid House world, everybody in the club or at a dance party was a star.

One national newspaper wrote about how police feared dance-party promoters (we were 'drug barons' again) with our 'tear-gas-wielding security teams with fierce dogs' and suggested that paratroopers should be dropped at the next bash to teach everybody present a hard lesson! OK, maybe it would be true to say that a small minority of people were prepared to fight for their right to party, but I know of only two occasions when riot squads and their vehicles were attacked by party people. They were normally E'd-up, fun-loving sorts.

However, the police had become accustomed to dealing with illegal parties and went all out to stop the events by any means necessary. In the process of carrying out their well-publicised raids a lot of innocent people got hurt. The tabloids backed them to the hilt, and I've put the following list of headlines together from cuttings in my scrap book. None of these headlines have been fabricated and they all appeared at various times in tabloids, regional newspapers or magazines around the country:

25,000 GO WILD ON ACID
SEND IN PARAS TO BEAT DRUGS EVIL
BUSTED! COPS' HUGE SWOOP FOILS ACID
  HOUSE PARTIES
FURY OVER M25 ACID HOUSE PARTY
THE ACID CRAZY DEVILS
TANKED-UP TERROR OF ACID INVADERS
CON BEHIND GIANT ACID HOUSE BASH
'LEGAL' ACEED SHOCK
ACID THUGS BLITZ COPS

TOP HEART HOSPITAL IN ACID TERROR

RIOT POLICE BATTLE ACID PARTY YOBBOS

'FIGHT ME,' ACID KING TELLS ROSS

ACID PARTY PLOTTER GETS 5 YEARS

8,000 IN ACID BASH INVASION AT VILLAGE

PHONE BAN HITS ACID HOUSE PARTIES

BEEB IN ACID FILM SNUB TO POLICE

COPS GIVE OK TO ACID PARTY

VILLAGE FURY OVER 13 HR ACID RAMPAGE

ACID WINS

GUNS SEIZED IN ACID HOUSE SWOOP

FURY AS ACID PARTY LOUTS GO ON
    RAMPAGE

DON'T COME TO THE PARTY SAY POLICE

231 HELD AT GIANT M-WAY ACID PARTY

LSD DEVILS

SMASH THESE EVIL ACID PARTIES

ACID GUARDS SET DEVIL DOGS ON RAID
    POLICE

CHAMP ON ACID

ACID HOUSE RIOT CHARGE

RAVING MAD

DAWN PATROL CAN PARTY ON

KIDS DEFY COPS

ACID PARTY KIDS LOSE £160,000 IN RIP OFF

END OF ACID LINE

FAMILIES HIT BY COPS' ACID BLOCKADE

ACID'S LAST STAND

DRIVERS' ACID MOB TERROR

ACID HOUSE DRUG KINGS ARE GUILTY

DRIVER IN ACID PARTY BLOCKADE

POLICE BLITZ FOILS THE ACID HOUSE PARTY
  NETWORK

DEVIL DOGS FIGHT ACID RAID COPS

ACID BOUNCERS HURT 16 COPS IN CS GAS
  RIOT ACID JAMS TUNNEL

CS GAS HEAVIES BEAT OFF ACID PARTY COPS

COPS BACK OFF IN ACID HOUSE BATTLE

ACID PARTY BOSS IS CLEARED

ANOTHER ACID CRACKDOWN

M25 ACID PARTY'S MR BIG DOES A BUNK TO
  COSTA DEL SOL AFTER £500,000 RIP OFF

BBC SNUBS POLICE OVER ACID PARTY

M1 ACID KIDS FOIL COPS IN DASH TO RAVE
  UP

ECSTASY – THE SUN CRACKS SECRET DRUG
  RAVE-UP IN HANGAR

ACID YOBS IN RIOT

JAIL FOR PARTY BOSSES

THE WAREHOUSE PARTY BOOM

DRUGS POLICE RAID NIGHT-CLUB

ACID PARTY CURB

POLICE BLOCK THE ACID PARTIES AND SAY
  BATTLE MAY BE OVER

POLICE TURN OFF THE ACID
20-HOUR ACID PARTY STORM
HOT-LINE ON ACID HOUSE
THIRTY ACID HOUSE REVELLERS ARRESTED
  AS POLICE JOIN FORCES
CLAMP ON ACID PARTIES
ACID HOUSE PLEA TO CONSERVATIVE PARTY
  POOPERS

DEMOLITION MEN

A special police squad known as the demolition men
were hand-picked to combat the rise of illegal dance
parties. Their central intelligence command centre
consisted of 27 senior officers whose brief was to gather
information on dance parties and anybody connected to
the organisations who promoted them. They compiled
databases and information packs with details of
promoters and their staff, and the packs were then sent
to police stations and councils around the country.

The name of every known person involved in the
staging of illegal events, addresses and telephone numbers
was logged into the department's central computer.
DJs, printers, flying teams, pirate radio stations, sound
and lighting crews, ticket outlets and agents were all
documented. They controlled Special Patrol Groups

(SPGs) around the country who were deployed for the sole purpose of closing down any dance party they came across.

The shop-a-promoter hotlines were manned 24 hours a day. Undercover cops would stand outside nightclubs, hanging around the people that were distributing flyers to clubbers, trying to listen out for information on promoters, the next big events, venue clues or anything else that could be of interest to the squad. Once they found out which events were taking place, and the meeting points, a full riot squad would be sent out armed with hit lists.

Gigs were placed in order of importance: the bigger events were stopped first, closely followed by some of the smaller gigs. The unit's success rate was very high and most events were stopped with the minimum of resistance. It wasn't the same as in the very early days, because in those early days the squads were not as organised as the promoters: on most occasions the police were taken completely by surprise and when the venue address was released the unit would rush to the site to be confronted by thousands of people.

Once the national squad was formed, life became a lot tougher for promoters, and this introduced a new aggressive breed of promoter and punter. When the police units were nice they were very nice, but when they were bad they were very bad. In my time of organising and attending illegal dance parties I've seen three full-on clashes with the department.

On one occasion an event in the country was stopped by the squad. There were hundreds of people walking along a dark, quiet road towards the party location. Several police vans blocked their path and around 70 officers stood in front of their vehicles with truncheons and shields in their hands. The punters' advance stopped short ten yards from the unit and the commanding gaffer ordered us to turn back or arrests would be made.

A group of geezers pushed their way through the crowd out to the front and started shouting obscenities at the policemen. The squad sprang into action and ran towards the group, which caused panic as everybody turned to run away. The officers starting hitting anyone they could. The stampede suddenly stopped and changed direction, running straight into the oncoming squad.

A battle commenced as the unit tried to hold their line. The commanding officer realised the seriousness of the attack and called for calm on a megaphone. After ten minutes of fighting it all calmed down, but everyone was still standing their ground. The officer told the crowd they could have the party if the violence ceased and the punters screamed with joy.

The unit stood aside as the group aggressively walked by. As we made our way to the party site, we heard a commotion behind us and looked around to see what was happening. The riot squad were now in their vans and driving slowly through the crowd. The last two vehicles were being attacked by a group of troublemakers who were hellbent on causing as much damage as they could. The crews jumped out of the two vans only to find themselves punched and kicked from all angles. They made it to the other vans and quickly escaped the danger area.

The abandoned vehicles were turned on their sides and set on fire and we scarpered from the hot-spot and across some fields until we reached the party site. There were about 4,000 people in attendance who danced until 7 a.m. The newspaper headlines the next day made things even harder for promoters and, because of this dark night, public opinion veered in favour of the law.

Not only did we have to deal with the government, Old Bill and Fleet Street: now the public had also turned against us. From that day, promoters were branded Public Enemy Number One. The police were given licence by the media and public to do whatever it took to bring promoters to trial, and crush a rebellion that they viewed as a threat. It took the police a while to gain control, but credit where credit is due: they did halt the rise of illegal gatherings. However, by then it was too late. The seed had been sown and the nation was already hooked on dance parties and House music.

THE NEW LAWS

The government soon wised up to the illegal party scene and introduced changes to the law to try to counteract promoters who were exploiting the 1982 Public Entertainment Act. One clause in that legislation had meant that promoters didn't need to apply for a music and dance licence for parties as long as tickets weren't on sale to the general public.

We exploited this loophole by selling membership cards for a fee and giving the party tickets away free. This was a perfectly legitimate arrangement. The Home Office fought these tactics by pushing local authorities into making use of the Private Places of Entertainment Act 1967, which required everyone arranging private parties to apply for licences. This was a huge blow to promoters and abruptly brought an end to the private-party loopholes, which in turn put a lot of people out of business.

The law did deter a few dodge organisations from staging events, but the main effect was to create a new breed of promoter, doorman and clubber. Now, when functions were planned everyone was hyped up to ensure the party went on. If the party was allowed to continue there wouldn't be any disturbances, but if the police tried to stop the event there would be a full-scale riot. One well-known promoter even publicly warned

Dibble: 'If you come in peace then peace unto them, but if you come in force it will rain down on you hard.'

This threat was published in a national newspaper and reflected the mood of the country's underground, but these events all took place *after* the sensationalised coverage in the national press. The parties were attracting dealers from all over the country who were motivated by the rich pickings of huge events. They didn't need prompting to stand up for their rights and as soon as they saw a roadblock all hell would break loose.

Promoters were held responsible for such disturbances and a new law allowed for summary fines of up to £20,000, a compulsory six-month prison sentence, and assets and profits in excess of £10,000 to be confiscated from promoters involved in staging illegal parties. This had the opposite effect from the one which was intended: it pushed promoters away from working with the police to find positive solutions and back underground again.

There were only a chosen few promoters who tried to organise legal gigs so a hundred or so promoters were left twiddling their thumbs with nothing to do. Unsurprisingly, a dark side to the party scene developed. Needless to say, we felt pretty pissed off with the government. After all, it was the Thatcherite era that had created the environment that was meant to encourage initiative and entrepreneurs like us.

The dance-music and party industry could have been worth millions to the government yet, instead, promoters were outlawed and turned into sinister gangsters or drug dealers by the media.

BULLSHITTERS

As well as credible organisers, the Acid House movement threw up untold tricksters. Chancers would go through the motions of staging an event by printing flyers with all the top DJs' names on and selling tickets in advance. Because of the rush to buy tickets, everyone would make sure they had a ticket one week before the bash. Thousands would be sold and on the night of the gig the 'promoters' would simply disappear with all the dosh.

Sometimes these dodge geezers would stage an event, but it would bear no relation to the one described on the ticket. There'd be no top DJs and no funfair, just a tiny, unsafe venue with a high risk of being closed down when inspected by the Old Bill. The promoters didn't give a shit: why should they care when they could dupe 30 to 40 grand in one hit? Promoting parties was better than drug dealing and, even if they were also dealers, they could make rich pickings at these events. There were just no risks involved for them.

When you could get ticket money in advance from the outlets, it helped organisers considerably. No party was ever guaranteed not to be stopped. If you had some of the cash in advance, at least you could pay off some of the expenses accumulated on staging the event, and try to construct a deal whereby the ticket holders kept their purchased tickets and used them at another event.

If we had some of the money it would help towards staging the next event, instead of running at a complete loss. We have personally lost around 70 grand because of parties being stopped. I know some promoters who lost thousands of pounds to impostors who turned up to ticket outlets pretending they'd organised the parties themselves.

Something had to be done, and so the outlets agreed with the promoters that legally binding contracts must be drawn up before big parties and signed by the promoter and the owner of the outlet. Only the named signatories could collect any money outstanding directly from the owner or manager, and even then there'd be a secret code. In any case, buying tickets well in advance became a thing of the past. Tickets wouldn't really start selling until two days before the event, but on the day of the party you could sell 3,000 tickets before 3 p.m. and continue to shift tickets through the night.

Because the gigs were illegal, normal concert-ticket agencies wouldn't touch us, which meant we had to find an easier alternative. Record shops and trendy clothing stores were great, and the more agents you had spread across the country, the better were the odds of selling more tickets. These guys sold more than the retail shops that opened all hours because they were mainly party people who knew loads of people who wanted tickets; they'd call us and buy 50 or so at one time.

We soon realised the value of these agents, and proposed a deal with each of them whereby we would print their name and number on our flyers. We'd give them 200 tickets at a time, then bike over more as needed. We built a vast national network of agents who, between them, could sell up to 5,000 tickets in three days. These guys were gold mines to promoters.

BLAGGERS

There's nothing I find more irritating than people stealing or leeching on to someone else's idea. In fact, it really pisses me off. During Genesis' history, at least three different groups of people used our name to promote their own two-bit parties.

There was one particular guy in south London who I met a couple of times when dropping off flyers or tickets. Let's call him Dick Ed. Now, I've always been an approachable type of person who listens to ideas or gives unknown DJs a shot at the big time.

At one stage I'd receive demo tapes virtually every day from DJs who wanted to play at our gigs. Dick Ed was one of these unknown DJs who was always babbling on about how good he was. According to him, he was the best.

I'd never book DJs without hearing a demo, although most of them don't like doing tapes for organisers. Nonetheless, I was a professional. No tape, no play: it was as simple as that. If the DJs have confidence in their set, where's the problem?

Dick Ed agreed to bring me a demo and we shook hands and went our separate ways. A couple of months later some shite A4 flyers hit the street billing a 'Genesis Mandela Peace Festival' in a venue somewhere in Dorking. What?! Genesis was our pride and joy, our treasure, and we'd worked mighty hard to build this reputation and even harder to maintain it. We'd been kidnapped at gunpoint, threatened with prison by Dibble and spent many a sleepless night handing out flyers outside clubs. We weren't about to let *anybody* get away with making money out of our sweat. We also had a good rep for staging fantastic events, not backstreet jobs. There was a contact number on the flyer and I rang it.

'Hello, is this Genesis?' I asked.

'Yes,' came the reply. 'Can I help you?'

'Is this the original Genesis?' I asked.

'Yes.'

'You must know me, then.'

'Why, who are you?'

'I'm the original Genesis,' I said.

'Is that Wayne?'

'Yes.'

'I'll tell you what, Wayne. I know where you live. This party is going on, or I'll fuck you up.'

Click. Before I had a chance to react, the guy had hung up. Wow, this geezer must be crazy! I wondered if he knew what he was dealing with. I called our security team to inform them of what was happening. I had the address of the venue, which was written in biro on the cardboard entrance ticket. We didn't know the culprits or where they came from, so we had to sit tight and wait for the night of the gig.

Meanwhile, we put the word out and tried to hunt down a name or some information that would lead us to the moody promoters. We also called the ticket outlets on his flyer and told them that this was a dodge party that was going to be closed down. I knew most of the outlets and had done business with them in the past, so it wasn't a problem to arrange. They stopped selling the tickets immediately and kept the money to be refunded to the purchasers.

Three days before the event I received an interesting phone call. The caller wouldn't tell me who he was but went on to give me the name and address we had been desperately hunting. Dick Ed! I couldn't believe it: the unknown DJ I had met a couple of months ago was responsible for this rip-off!

I had taken time out of a busy schedule to hear what the geezer had to say and then promised him I would listen to his tape and maybe give him a shot at playing a set. I didn't even know him, and he'd not only nicked our name but threatened to bring trouble to my doorstep. I was really angry and called the number straight away. It rang a few times before I heard his voice.

'Genesis. Hello.'

'Is that Dick Ed? I know where you live, and I'll be outside your house any minute now. You'd better get ready.' Click.

Two minutes later, my phone rang.

'Listen, Wayne. I don't want any trouble. I'm sorry I said what I did.'

'Tell me to my face. I'll be there any second.'

'I'm not at my house. I'm at my friend's place. I really don't want it, man, honest. Can we make a deal?'

'No. You listen: there's no party going on. Do you understand?'

'Yeah.'

'You'd better take all the money you took from the ticket outlets back tomorrow. You're in deep shit, and if you haven't done it by Saturday morning the party's over for you. Full stop.' Click.

The last thing I wanted was trouble. This was a peaceful, non-violent dance movement, but even so we couldn't allow people to nick our ideas and name like that. Luckily for Dick Ed, he did everything he was instructed and I never ever saw him again.

Nonetheless, on the Monday following the event we were dumbstruck when we read an article in a national newspaper that was headlined: 'Acid Kids Duped in £160,000 Party Con'. The sensationalised story by an unnamed reporter claimed up to 10,000 people had forked out £16 per head for the Genesis Mandela Peace Festival, which never took place. It went on to say that 130 officers had blocked all roads leading to the field in Dorking. Partygoers were reportedly turned away from the site and expressed anger at being ripped off by the promoters.

Now, as far as we know, only a small number of tickets were sold by the agents and outlets. We'd got to the main ticket outlets before the event and they can't have sold more than a hundred units in advance. In those days it was virtually impossible to sell 10,000 units before the event and none of the established promoters had ever achieved this incredible feat. It was simply another example of tabloid anti-dance-party propaganda.

Other bods would go around claiming to be the organisers of Genesis or other party companies. There was one long-haired guy from a party organisation called In Search of Space who fitted this equation perfectly. He did a bit of running about for us, stuff like picking up the drinks from the wholesaler, then while my partners and I took care of business he would be standing on the stage waving and thanking everyone for coming.

After a couple of events we had to sack the geezer because he was driving us mad and we didn't need the stress. He would go to 7–11 for more supplies, and come back claiming that he had 500 people following him who had been en route somewhere else but he'd convinced them to come here instead. The security that helped him bring the stuff in said he came with two cars. We had enough of the bollocks and he had to go.

There were only ever three of us who ran Genesis from the beginning until it all ended in 1990, yet I've met loads of people who say: 'Didn't you run Genesis with Tom, Dick or Harry?' And to think some of the bods making these wild claims were our pals! I guess they didn't plan on us ever meeting the people they said it to. I used to tell them to say: 'Wayne said that you've never had anything to do with them and never will.' That ought to shut them up! In truth, I was just embarrassed for them.

RECORDED PHONE-LINE MESSAGES

Recorded phone-line messages had soon made meeting points a thing of the past. This was good because they had always brought Dibble down to the venues too quickly. If the police did close off the meet, there was no way we could stop people going into that area, which was a bummer if you'd found another venue just a few miles away.

A recorded message was the perfect tool in our fight against getting our parties closed. Nobody had to even leave their house to get venue details, which would be released at a scheduled time (when the venue was 100% ready). Party people would then converge on the motorways, A roads and town streets simultaneously. People from different parts of the country would make their way to the venue, armed with a road atlas, information telephone numbers, tickets and membership cards.

As has already been mentioned, it was virtually impossible to block all routes to the secret locations, but it got to a point when even blockades didn't deter people from getting into a warehouse, especially when they could hear the music coming from inside the building.

The police would sometimes let the party continue with the people that were already there but stop anyone else from entering. Normally there were more party people than Old Bill so people would just park their car up and continue on foot, which gave them more chance of getting into the gig.

Mailing list telephone lines were also introduced, which meant you could leave your details on a recorded telephone line 24 hours a day. You would then be sent up-to-the-minute information, and even if you didn't go to clubs much you'd still receive news of future events before the flyers had hit the street. There would be a huge party on practically every Saturday and most promoters would use the phone lines and radio stations to announce venue details.

Because of this situation, the authorities soon decided to ban the use of recorded telephone lines for dance-party promoters. The ICSTIS (Independent Committee for the Supervision of Standards of Telephone Information Services) faxed the following letter to companies around the country:

Notice to Service Providers

At its meeting of 10 October 1989 the ICSTIS considered the use of premium-rate telephone services to inform callers of the location of so-called Acid House Parties.

Consequently, the committee desires to communicate the following advice:

Communications on the premium-rate telephone network used for the promotion of mass gatherings such as the so-called Acid House Parties, as presently arranged with minimum amount of notice of the venue, will constitute a breach of the ICSTIS Code of Practice.

18 October 1989

So the party phone lines scam came to an end. We could still use them for other services, but not for anything to do with venue locations.

PIRATE RADIO

Ongoing legal changes meant that promoters had to be more discreet and organise their promotional campaigns further upfront and, before long, pirate radio was playing a major role in the promotion of music-and-dance parties. These stations broadcast 24 hours a day, seven days a week, and played nothing but House music. Everybody, particularly in London, would be glued to their local pirates, listening out for news of events, record releases or party cancellations. All the dance-party promoters used the stations to advertise their gigs. The commercials had to be no more than 40 seconds. Specially recorded ads were played on the hour every hour. They used to charge £100–£200 per week, depending on who you were dealing with.

There were maybe seven or eight pirates operating on the FM frequency, all within millimetres of each other. Sunrise, Fantasy and Centreforce were a few of the more popular stations in the early days. The DJs had all the music you heard at parties and so tuning into the radio was something everybody did, any chance they got.

Whenever I listened to the pirates, I'd have the RECORD button constantly paused, waiting for that wicked track that I'd heard Carl Cox playing the previous night. The pirates were marketed solely to party people and so, if promoters needed to make an urgent announcement, we'd call the studio directly. Within seconds, the DJs would then repeat what they'd been told over the airwaves.

This was another useful tool in our race against the police and provided us with instant access to the public at large. The pirate boys had it completely sussed and had transmitters plotted all over London. As soon as the Department of Trade and Industry found one transmitter and temporarily cut them off, another one would be broadcasting within minutes. The DTI couldn't win.

The pirate guys were as organised as we were, and good luck to them. They were earning good money back in 1989 but, if they weren't consistent, us promoters wouldn't use them. Of course, we of all people knew that things could always go wrong, but at the end of the day our objectives were to promote the gigs. We weren't going to pay money out to a station to be cut off for weeks, but if it took them a day to organise we could cope with that.

The proper firms had it sorted. If they lost one transmitter they would switch to another, and if that one went down too, there'd be another fallback. The switchover wouldn't usually last longer than an hour, then it would all be back to normal. The commercials that the pirates broadcast on the hour could last for fifteen minutes because there were so many of them. Each promoter was paying at least £100, so it was in the station's best interests to be organised and stay on top of things.

I went to one of the studio set-ups on the top floor of a tower block. Its doorway was cemented with bits of concrete and iron, wired up to car batteries. When the council, police or DTI tried to go anywhere near the studio entrance, the door would be electrified, sending shock spasms through anybody who touched it. We had to get on to the roof via the stairway and then practically abseil down on to the balcony. It was pretty scary shit.

The DJs used to lower their record boxes down on a rope before they could climb into the studio. A lot of the guys were so used to doing this death-defying feat that they would be jumping and swinging into the window. After I saw that, I would happily give them my money because they would actually risk life and limb to ensure that the show went on.

To a large degree, the stations were responsible for bringing House music out of the clubs and parties and exposing the brand-new sound to the masses. One summer day in 1989 we were listening to a pirate station and a DJ was playing a wicked set. Then the DJ announced that the DTI and a police squad were trying to break the fully secured studio door down. He was telling everyone to keep the vibe alive, and continue dancing no matter what. Listening intently to the broadcast, our hearts went out to them. We faintly heard some shouting before the needle was dragged across the record and a loud, deep voice started speaking.

'Good evening, listeners,' it said. 'This is the police. I'm afraid to say this station has reached the end of the road. I just want to say what a good job our officers have done on this warm summer evening. We're going to play one last record which is dedicated to my team, our colleagues down at the station who are all listening, the officers out there fighting crime on the streets of London, and Acid party promoters. We want you all to remember that Big Brother is always watching. We've brought a record with us especially for this occasion and it's the theme from *Hill Street Blues:* the Scotland Yard remix. This is DC Jones on the wheels of steel playing the last record you'll ever hear on this station.'

On another occasion we were listening to a station when the DJ announced that his car had been stolen and described the make, model, colour and registration. He asked anyone who spotted the car to report the sighting to the police immediately. Within an hour, not only had someone spotted the motor but the suspect was in protective custody and the DJ had recovered the vehicle.

Another pirate announcement that I heard said: 'This is a message to the geezers who nicked my motor. If there's even a scratch on that bodywork you are going to regret ever setting eyes on it. I hope you like my friends, because they're going to bring you to the studio. This, ladies and gentlemen, is a fine example that crime sometimes doesn't pay!' I don't know what happened to the thief but, given the choice, I bet he'd have preferred to get nicked ...

ACID HOUSE GOES ORBITAL

The M25 played a major role in getting party people from all around the country together on one route.

It was easy enough to set roadblocks up on inner-London roads but to do so on motorways was virtually impossible. So, our struggle went orbital.

The key to ensuring the party would go ahead as planned was to locate a venue in the Home Counties, or just within the M25. Then you'd name two service stations as the meeting points, making sure they weren't too close together. When the service station car parks were full, promoters would send someone to head a convoy to the venue, which could easily contain as many as 3,000 cars. We found that if you did this in London the police would block certain routes and begin splitting everyone up. This worked in their favour because, once the crowds were dispersed, the police would close the party down and confiscate the equipment.

Soon, at least 25,000 party animals would be converging on the M25 each weekend, searching for a party to attend and go radio rental. You would instantly recognise your fellow revellers. Their car stereos were at full-blast, their heads were bopping and they were constantly on the look out for other party people. Once you'd established contact, the first words spoken were invariably: 'Where's the party, mate?'

Most of the time nobody knew where they were going. You either followed other cars, or else your map. You could be on the motorway for hours and still not find the party, and you'd end up telephoning the recorded-information line several times for clues you may have missed on previous calls.

However, the best buzz of all was driving in convoy to the event, especially if they were heading in the right direction. You'd start off with ten cars, and as you hit the motorways cars would join the trail of vehicles or drive side by side. Because the venue address was released at a set time, everybody would converge on the roads pretty much simultaneously.

One night we were on a major motorway en route to a party outside London. There must have been 500 cars riding in a convoy in the slow and middle lanes, and we travelled at speeds of less than 40 mph, so as not to lose anyone. It was a real adrenaline rush to look in your mirror and see nothing but headlights, stretching back as far as the eye could see.

We were among the first twenty cars, so we could see what was ahead. In the far distance we spotted blue and red flashing lights – and a lot of them. As we drew closer, we could see that it was a roadblock. The Old Bill had actually blocked a major motorway and the blockade was six cars across and three deep, with about 30 officers standing in front of their vehicles.

The police were giving us the hand signal to stop so we slowed to a crawl and came to a halt. Everyone started getting out of their cars and walking towards the blockade. The police were yelling at us to get back in our vehicles. Nobody was listening, and by now there were 300 people standing at the head of the convoy. One officer picked up a megaphone and told us that the party had been stopped and there was another roadblock ten miles ahead.

The officer said that we all had to turn around at this junction and go back to wherever we'd come from. Fuck that! We stood defiantly on the roofs of our cars and began to clap and somebody shouted: 'Street party!' A loud cheer echoed into the night sky and music began blasting from all the cars. We were dancing and clapping in the middle of a motorway. It was a full-on road party (the Reclaim the Streets promoters would have been proud of us!).

The police didn't know what to do. Although we were defying their orders, nobody was acting in a threatening manner. It wasn't a potential riot situation; in fact it was the other motorists who were angry and doing their nut at the Old Bill. Fifteen minutes later the police opened the roadblock and let us through. Then, as we approached the second block further down the road, the cars just moved to one side. The party hadn't been stopped and 6,000 people turned up.

On another occasion the police blocked an A road two minutes from the party venue. We were so close that we could see the party's flashing lights across a country field. Determined to reach the event, people began parking on the hard shoulder and making their way across marshlands towards the lights. There were about 50 policemen with dogs, and 2,000 ticket-holders. In the end, Dibble had no choice but to unblock the road. We got to the party thrilled to bits that we'd made it: we'd been rushing, sitting in the car, for over an hour.

Two hours later it was announced that the police were towing away the cars that had been parked on the hard shoulder. Scores of people left to check their motors and returned half an hour later to say that about 25 tow-trucks were taking the cars away. That night, over a hundred cars were taken to various police pounds around the motorway.

And the police operations didn't end there. Service stations around the M25 were also blocked by riot squads. However, it wasn't just partygoers who were trapped by the roadblocks: everyone in the service station was stopped from leaving. Although ticket-holders expressed their anger to Dibble at being penned in and having their civil rights obliterated, the threat of violence was nonexistent.

Admittedly, a group of over a thousand people will generate a lot of noise but there was never a threat of physical violence. The ticket-holders didn't need to cause trouble: ordinary road users gave the riot squads enough abuse without our aid. The roadblocks could last from one to five hours and nobody was allowed in or out. Can you imagine the tension that this caused?

We party people were used to this kind of treatment because the media and the authorities had basically given the police licence to do with us as they pleased. In our eyes, this was just another weekend of catch-and-chase. However, the other road users were outraged by the police's measures to stop people reaching their destinations. They often expressed resentment, and practically started violence between themselves and the squads. Then, the following day, newspapers would publish stories of how families were trapped in service stations with thousands of drugged-up criminals, fearing for their lives and the safety of their children. It was the kind of unfairness we soon became used to. But would the authorities have agreed to mount a similar assault against more 'decent', accepted members of society?

CHEMICAL REACTIONS

It's impossible to separate the Acid House scene from Ecstasy and the other drugs that soundtracked it. In fact, a lot of people would argue that the scene WAS the drugs and that anybody who had never taken Ecstasy could never begin to understand what was going on.

Now, I'm not condoning or recommending drug use in this book, but I can't deny that chemicals have given me a lot of fun, and memorable, moments.

At one stage Keith and I got into the habit of dropping large amounts of Acid and doing absolutely radio rental things. Keith was going through a phase of spiking drinks with microdots, which was absolute murder. I'd go around his place in the morning and get offered tea and toast, then half an hour after I'd eaten the munch, he'd say, 'Are you buzzing?' He caught me a few times, until I got wise and never accepted food or drink from him.

Keith bought 100 microdots so that he could spike as many people in one night as possible. It reached a stage where he was throwing the small seedlike trips at tables crammed with drinks. Nobody knew which glasses were contaminated or who was the culprit responsible for the unexpected headfuck.

Anyway, we were on the sniff one night when Keith challenged anyone to drop a dot and parachute from an aeroplane. He even offered a grand to the lunatic that did it, and I said that I'd also bung a grand into the kitty for the person with balls enough to jump.

We'd pulled some gorgeous Italian models a few weeks earlier and they'd been with us ever since our meeting. They thought we were crazy and, looking back on it, we were totally off our nut. It was the 'what do you give a man with everything?' scenario. We constantly lived such a high life that it all became boring and so we just constantly thought of ways to achieve the ultimate rush.

They say money doesn't bring you happiness, and I agree, but it is a good way of keeping the mind occupied. However, I certainly wouldn't contemplate now doing the dumb things we did back then. Nobody was willing to accept the aeroplane challenge, but secretly I had always yearned to jump from a plane. Fuck it! I threw the gauntlet down and challenged Keith to jump with me; he accepted without a second's hesitation. There was no money at stake – just red-blooded pride. A pal of ours named Touch had recently passed his pilot's test and treated himself to a twin-engine aeroplane. He used to hang out with a guy, Steve, who had spent seven years in the parachute regiment and done over 300 jumps. Between them, they had enough equipment for six people to take the plunge.

We got Touch on the blower there and then and made an arrangement to meet at a private airfield a few days later. On the morning of the jump we dropped a microdot at 10 a.m. Our terrifying ordeal was scheduled for 1 p.m., so we wanted to be sure that we were at peaking point before our big test.

Some friends and the Italian girls came with us to witness our death-defying feat and we drove in convoy to the airfield where we met Touch and Steve. A quick glance at the planes in the hangar started twitches inside my gut. I looked over at the runway, where four magnificent rainbows stretched from one side of the sky to the other. I couldn't point this out to the others, because at this point I started rethinking what I was about to attempt and felt so nervous that I couldn't speak.

Steve was a professional and took us to a patch of grass where he showed us some breakfalls for when we were coming in to land. We went over the emergency pull-tag procedures in case things went horribly wrong. Keith was in hysterics but I could tell it was a nervous laugh. He was just as scared as me.

What the fuck am I doing here? I was asking myself. Let's just swallow my pride. What is there to prove? An internal war was waging, but the moment of truth had come.

'OK, lads, zero hour approaches. Let's get the kit on,' said Steve.

We couldn't tell him we were tripping because he'd have gone mad and not allowed us to jump. We went to the plane in the hangar. Keith, Steve and I were the only ones who were going to go for it. The plane looked frighteningly small. Were we really going to do this?

Steve strapped us into our chutes and I heard every G-clip being snapped into place. Touch started the plane's twin propellers and a swarm of butterflies in my stomach sprang to life. I felt an urge to quote a Tom Cruise line from the movie *Top Gun* and turned to Keith. 'I feel the need, the need for speed,' I said, luckily waking him from the trance of his tab. We gave it loads to our pals and climbed into the body of the metal dragonfly. Steve told us not to forget to close our mouths as we fell because the G-force would have us dribbling all over our faces.

There were just four of us on the plane. It tore along the runway and took flight. It was a clear afternoon with blue skies, so I tried to focus on the beauty of Mother Earth. But the drugs were too strong and I kept seeing the maddest images. At one stage there was a huge Michelin man hopping from cloud to cloud; each move that he made freeze-framed across the sky. He stopped and looked directly at me and I closed my eyes. He was sitting cross-legged on a magic carpet and mimicking my facial expressions. Then, suddenly, the padded balloon-man clapped his hands and disappeared in a cloud of pink smoke.

I opened my eyes and looked around the aircraft. The occupants were all staring at me, and Steve asked if I was OK.

Keith was having a laughing fit. 'He's nervous, can't you tell?' he said, laughing at me.

The most important thing was not to give the game away. 'Of course I'm all right,' I said. Keith was holding it down but I knew him like a brother and he was shitting himself. The colours in the sky were so intense that I felt energy vibrating from them.

Steve was looking out of the window and gave us the thumbs-up signal. 'The drop zone at 7,000 feet is approaching.'

I didn't want to jump first and neither did Keith so we flicked a coin. I lost. Before the horror could truly sink in I stood up, hooked my backpack to the static line and moved towards the exit.

Standing by the small door and looking down towards the ground affected my breathing. Every muscle in my body tightened up. Any slight movement could send me flying through the air. My grip on the metal handle by the side of the door wouldn't loosen. The jump procedure was for the jumpmaster to tap the arm that was holding the handle as a signal to jump. Steve did so, and my fear seemed to neutralise for a brief moment. Then, suddenly, point break: a rush of 100% pure adrenaline, driven by one of the strongest hallucinogenics known to man!

Once I had jumped out of the plane, several things happened simultaneously. First there was an incredible sense of weightlessness as I got sucked into the slipstream behind the plane. I was tossed around and couldn't focus properly. The land and the plane quickly flickered on the edges of my vision.

The static line pulled the chute out and it suddenly felt as if somebody was ripping my back off. I wished I was at home. My body was still in the same position as when I'd jumped and I was falling at a high velocity, reaching speeds of 80 mph. It seemed like for ever, but in reality it was merely seconds before everything slowed down and the force of the harness got stronger and stronger as the chute cushioned a large chunk of air and opened up fully. For a split second I was motionless and beheld the unique and spectacular beauty of nature. Now I was bouncing my way down, like a puppet on long strings, and the noise of the aeroplane faded until absolute silence reigned.

I looked up for Keith but my chute was obscuring my view. However, I could see Steve and he was looking good, weaving from side to side. I wanted to try a few moves myself but the ground seemed to be closing in fast and, moving at high speed, I shaped my body into the landing position and prepared for impact.

My face must have donned a look of total fear because the green grass seemed to be approaching far too fast. Suddenly I hit, safely, and rolled over. A minute later Keith landed near to me and fell over. A freak breeze filled his chute and dragged him along the dirt. I got a vision of him being seriously hurt, but even so couldn't stop myself from creasing up in laughter. Keith sprang up straight away and then Steve came down and landed on his feet – flash git!

Keith and I were going berserk. We've done it, and we're alive! Yeeesss!!

To completely understand this inspiring but terrifying experience, try to multiply a normal parachute jump by 50, then throw in some extra-special effects for good measure. We were heroes, man! Top buzzers, extreme to the max! The girls gave us a full Italian job that night, but when the LSD wore off I made a solemn oath not to jump tripping from a plane again. I told my mum what I had done (leaving out the tab bit, obviously) and she nearly fainted. Keith and I never challenged each other again – fuck that! Life is a learning process and I strongly wish to continue it ...

FIRST TRIP

I took my first trip in 1984 when LSD was a lot stronger than the crap around today. Just like Ecstasy in 1988, it was purer and cleaner than it is now. I dropped it with some friends who had tripped before on many occasions.

We went to score the Superman blotting paper in a large abandoned bus station in Hackney. My friends had scored some strong shit there only recently, so we knew there was some. The whole building resembled a scene from *Mad Max: Beyond Thunderdome*. Hippies had taken over the depot and made it into their temporary home. There were coaches and caravans scattered around the place, small children were playing, bonfires blazing and a flower power family were doing t'ai chi exercises.

We walked into one of the building's offices and found the people inside it sitting in a circle on cushions. The room was cluttered with spiritual paraphernalia from around the globe. Our new hosts invited us to sit down and join them on their magical journey throughout the cosmos. The aroma of incense filled the air and we were just in time for a toke on the massive joint that was going round.

We bought a trip each and washed it down with a pils. Our hosts were already tripping and totally chilled. After the big spliff had gone around three times, we quickly got stoned. At this stage, the LSD was starting to take effect. One of the hippies was advising us to think nothing but good thoughts and think of the trip as a life-enhancing experience. He told me to look out for colours and the energy fields around plants and life forms.

I was eighteen and from the hood and, although my mother raised us with all the love a child could ask for, I really didn't give a bollocks about energy fields and the cosmos. I wanted to see mad, terrifying hallucinations, the kind that send your pulse racing and your heart pounding. I wanted the full Monty: a hands-on virtual-reality experience in a twilight world.

However, the good karma being produced by our environmentally sussed buddies managed to keep the horrors at bay. I did learn something that day, and that was how to appreciate a really good trip. Dropping a tab in a warehouse party with untold people having it around you is a trip in itself, but this was different: these guys seemed to be having astrally projected group meetings on another plane! I reckon the hippies of the Sixties could teach us a thing or two about evolution and spirituality.

I did see Conan the Barbarian in full Technicolor, however. He stepped out of the wall, and although my sight was blurred I could still clearly see him. He raised his sword and swung it around in slow motion. He was sweating and didn't smile. As soon as I blinked, he disappeared.

On the way home we walked through a park called London Fields. When I was a child growing up in the area, I heard stories of bubonic-plague victims being buried deep beneath the park's green grass. Tales of people being harassed by bad spirits were commonplace. Unless you crossed the green with a group of friends, you would hardly dare think of walking across the grass unarmed, at night, on your own.

My mates and I were winding each other up and trying to bring out the dark side in the Acid. It was 2 a.m. so the park was dead quiet, except for us lot laughing and acting like prats. There was a railway bridge and some alleyways on the other side of the green, and a speeding train was passing over the visible section of the bridge. It caught my attention because I couldn't hear any sound coming from the train.

The train was only a few hundred yards away, so we should definitely have been able to hear it. I pointed it out to the others and we tried our hardest to listen out for any engine noises coming from the train's direction. We looked at each other and burst into laughter, then when we looked back at the track the train had gone.

Standing where the train had been was the dark shadow of a tall man. He was facing our way. We walked towards the eerie figure to check if it was real, but as we got closer he just vanished into thin air, which freaked us out. We hightailed it out of the Fields as quickly as possible, tripping one another up on the way.

For eight solid hours we laughed hysterically for no apparent reason and, in the morning, my stomach ached like mad. I was told it was because of the speed in the Acid. I've never liked speed and have only sampled it once. It's a horrible drug with bad comedowns. The only time I took it, I sniffed a line of top-quality stuff called Pink champagne and almost chewed my tongue to bits. I ground my teeth together pretty much nonstop for six hours.

The speed comedown was like nothing I had ever experienced before. I had terrible pains in my stomach and felt really depressed. I called one of my pals, who was a speed freak, and asked him if it was normal for me to be feeling like shit. He said it was how most people felt after a night on the whizz.

I've always viewed taking drugs as a recreational pastime to enjoy with your mates. I can't see the point in taking a stimulant that makes you physically or mentally unstable the following day. I've never gone anywhere near speed since and never will, and the same goes for smack. There are some things I just don't want to know about.

ENIGMA

I shall never forget the day I witnessed an ex-girlfriend, Zoe, have a bad trip. I mean, I've heard some wild stories in my time but this one is definitely up there with the best of them. While out and about one night, I was introduced to a pretty girl whom I immediately clicked with. One thing led to another, and we spent the following two weeks together.

As we were getting used to each other, and covering just about every conversational topic on the planet, the subject of LSD came up and we discussed our past tripping experiences. She had had her last tab a year before and thoroughly enjoyed it. Around then, there were some really strong tabs called Pink Floyds on the market. Zoe suggested that we trip together, but only if we found a Floyd. I agreed, and we spent the next two weeks looking for someone who sold them. Finally, we tracked someone down and bought three at a fiver each. As we pulled up back at Zoe's place, my pal Danny was just coming out of the block, and I invited him to come and trip with me and Zoe.

Zoe was a musician who always played loud music. She lived and breathed music. She shared a flat with her good friend, Paula, who was a couple of years older than her. Paula didn't take LSD but had no objections to us doing it. Danny was up for it, and we all dropped the tiny square of blotting paper around midnight.

Within ten minutes we were laughing hysterically. My cheeks and stomach were hurting from laughing so much. Now, I've had loads of trips in the past but I knew that this one was very strong and could feel the effects intensifying. This was going to be a top buzz and, as we planned to stay in for the evening and nobody was going to see us, it didn't matter how messy we got.

Twenty minutes had passed when Zoe got up and left the room. Danny and I were still laughing our heads off for no apparent reason, but Zoe wasn't gone for very long before I began to wonder where she'd disappeared to. I got up to see where she'd gone and looked into her bedroom. The light was off and Seal's track 'Killer' was playing softly in the background. Zoe had thousands of pounds' worth of recording equipment in her bedroom. The little red lights were all on and it looked like an aeroplane cockpit. Turning the light on, I saw Zoe huddled up in the corner on top of her bed. I asked her if she was OK and she said no. She was shaking uncontrollably so I went over and hugged her.

Zoe looked at me, said 'Oh, it's you. I love you' and grabbed hold of my head and bit me hard on the cheek. She then apologised and wrapped her arms around me. Seconds later, she bit me again. Although I knew she was a horny chick, this wasn't sexual. It was far more serious than it seemed.

I called out to Paula for some orange juice. The vitamin C in the juice brings the drug down, but it's a long process. However, orange was the only source of vitamin C available to us. She brought a glassful, which I tried to make Zoe drink, but she kept biting the glass really hard. I thought it would break, so I took it from her. She began screaming 'Enigma, enigma!' at the top of her voice and called out for Paula while telling me to leave the room.

My main goal was to calm Zoe down but this really wasn't working, so I went into the front room where Danny and Paula were sitting. I told Paula that she was having a bad trip and to try to make her drink some orange. By now, Zoe was screaming her head off. Danny and I were staring silently at one another. I was thinking: Shit, I can't believe this is happening. Paula was in the room with her for a matter of minutes when Zoe suddenly shouted at her to get out. I heard a loud crash and bang, and headed for the bedroom. Paula came out and told me to leave Zoe alone, adding that she did this sort of thing quite a lot.

In my experience of taking trips, you don't leave somebody on their own when they are having a bad one: fuck that! I tried the door and found it was now locked. I could hear her crying inside, and booted the wooden door in. To my horror, Zoe had smashed up her recording equipment and was sitting on the floor completely naked. There was some kind of solid plastic thing in her hand, with which she was scraping herself across the chest. Blood was seeping from her wounds, and the situation was critical enough for me to decide that we had to call an ambulance.

By now, Zoe was really trying to hurt herself – and me. I let go of one of her arms for a moment and she scratched me down the face. My whole cheek stung because sweat was running into the bloody lines on my face. I had to hold both of her arms tight to keep us from even greater damage. The recording equipment was the most important thing in Zoe's life, but she had really gone to town on smashing it to pieces. There was even a chair embedded in the mixing desk. I didn't particularly care about her stuff, however. My main concern was to get her better. I knew I had to get her to hospital.

Holding Zoe down on the bed with all my strength, I told Paula to call an ambulance and tell them she was having a bad trip. Danny came walking into the bedroom and I yelled at him to get out. My girlfriend was naked: I didn't want anyone to see her like this. Danny just looked at me oddly and ran out of the front door of the flat.

I shouted to Paula to help put some clothes on her before the ambulance came, but she just stood at the door, staring at us. Zoe, her best friend, had lost it, but Paula was doing nothing to help her. Every time I let Zoe go she would punch me in the face or headbutt the wall. She kept screaming 'Enigma' and other things that made no sense to me. I couldn't believe Paula wasn't helping me. I was tripping off my nut while all this was going on, but still somehow managing to focus on what was happening. Then Paula said, 'Don't worry about getting her dressed. Just take her down the hospital as she is.' Anger filled my body and I wanted to let go of Zoe and clump her, except that hitting women isn't my thing. Friendship is a serious thing and Paula had just miserably failed a big test.

I tried to dress Zoe in some tracksuit bottoms, but she was kicking and moving around too much. Paula simply went into the front room and stayed there. After an hour, the emergency services turned up and the ambulanceman walked into the bedroom, which by now was a total mess, with virtually everything broken. The ambulanceman surveyed the scene. I had huge gouges and teeth marks in my cheeks, and Zoe was naked with blood trickling down her breasts. He said there was no way he could take her as she was and we'd have to telephone the police. I didn't mind getting the Old Bill involved, but how could he say he wasn't taking her to hospital? I looked at him with blood running down my face, and said, 'You ARE taking her, mate!'

The ambulanceman could tell by the dark look in my eyes that I was at breaking point. He agreed to take her, and we tried to pick her up. Zoe had always been a strong girl, but now she was tripping she had super-strength. Quickly, I took hold of her legs while the medic grabbed her arms. Placing a blanket over her body, we began to carry her to the ambulance.

Everybody in the whole block of flats seemed to be standing by their windows or outside their front door, watching Zoe screaming, kicking and punching. We got her into the vehicle and, as there was only one paramedic, I had to hold her down in the back of the ambulance. The hospital was ten minutes away and she screamed constantly for the whole time. By now I was genuinely worried for her sanity. When we arrived at casualty, four porters had to be called to carry her inside. They were amazed: here was a beautiful woman, completely naked, going utterly apeshit and yelling about world peace, for some reason. We carried her into a curtained cubicle, where the porters put her down and left us alone.

Three doctors came in with an injection to reduce the effect of the LSD. We all had to pin her down before they could administer the medication. Then the doctors left me alone with Zoe again. She was still going mental and I had to hold her arms the whole time. While all this was going on, I was hallucinating on my own LSD trip. Everything I looked at started to change colour. Then, suddenly, the sound of Zoe screaming snapped me out of it: she was screaming 'Fuck me! Fuck me!' and every other obscenity you can think of. I tried to shut her up, but it was impossible.

The doctors came back into the cubicle to give Zoe another injection and a bad thing happened. One of the nurses was short and not exactly an oil painting. As I loosened my grip on Zoe's wrist for just a second, she suddenly screamed 'You ugly dwarf!' and punched the nurse full in the face.

I grabbed Zoe's arm to make sure it didn't happen again, and I couldn't apologise enough to the nurse: her face was red-raw where she'd been hit. She was cool about it, and approached us for the second time. Wham! Zoe kicked her hard in the legs and the poor nurse fell over and immediately called for help.

About seven nurses now came running in and took hold of Zoe's arms and legs. The doctor then gave her another injection, at which Zoe told him he was gorgeous and kept calling for him to come back. She calmed down a bit now, but was still trying to hurt herself at every opportunity.

By now my arms were aching like mad, I had sweat soaking through my clothes and was tripping off my nut. The funny thing was how focused I remained and that I knew exactly what was going on: they were trying to preserve the sanity and safety of my girlfriend. I fully understood what the doctors were trying to achieve even though everything else was going haywire. Colours were changing, walls moving, and I could hear every single sound in casualty. In the cubicle next to ours was a man who, by the sound of it, was in serious trouble. At one point his heart machine stopped and around ten medics went in to try to resuscitate him. I could hear women crying and being comforted by sobbing men. I knew that one thing was for sure: everyone must have heard Zoe's screams. I felt so ashamed. We were two young, healthy people who were in casualty only because one of us was having a bad trip. We were wasting the time of doctors who could be treating genuinely sick people.

A telephone rang and a doctor answered it and said there was nobody called Wayne in casualty. I told the doc that it was me and he handed me the phone. It was Danny calling to see if we were OK. I told him that Zoe had quietened down but I was now tripping big time and needed to see a friendly face. He said he was on the way and would only take fifteen minutes.

Meanwhile, Zoe was in a deep sleep and, for the first time in five hours, I was able to take a rest. I sat in the waiting room, reflecting on what we were going through and wondering if Zoe would be affected by the delay in bringing her down from the drug. Half an hour passed, then, at 5.30 a.m., a scream rang around the hospital corridors. I rushed back to Zoe's cubicle.

She was awake and rolling around on the floor, shouting my name. I turned her over on to her back and held her arms. She was possessed like the girl from *The*

Exorcist and kept yelling obscenities as loud as possible. There was a drip inserted into her arm and every time I loosened her grip she'd try to twist it around in her arm. I was terrified because I knew if she ruptured her vein we'd be in serious shit.

The head doctor came back in and said that they had already given Zoe the maximum possible dose of sedative according to normal medical guidelines. He called a senior doctor at another hospital to ask whether it was safe to give her any more, and was told to go ahead with extreme caution. An army of doctors arrived and gave her yet another injection.

She finally fell asleep and I was relieved that she was out like a baby. The doctors wanted to keep her in for observation. I left my jacket by her side so that, when she woke up in hospital, she wouldn't be too shocked and would see something she could connect with me and know I was still there.

Danny had arrived and was sitting in the waiting room. I asked him why he'd left me at the house. He said that when he'd walked, while tripping, into the room where Zoe and I were struggling with each other he'd thought I was raping her. He'd decided to get out as soon as possible, flagged a taxi down and made his way home. While in transit, he'd seen speeding police cars going in the direction of where he'd just come from, and thought they were coming for me! By the time he got home he was in a panic. It took him five hours to calm down and think rationally. At which point, he realised that I would never do something like that and rang the hospital.

Zoe was safely tucked up in bed by now. When we left the hospital and I stepped out into the cold air, the trip, which had been lying dormant for a while, went straight to my head. I was temporarily blinded by a thick coat of snow that covered everything in sight. I thought I had died and gone to heaven. Walking through the 'snow' was like floating on clouds, and everything was so bright I could hardly see. Danny shook me out of it and took me to my car, which he had picked up earlier from Zoe's place. When he started the engine and pressed the gas we heard a snapping sound. The accelerator cable had broken because of the ice.

The traffic on the roads was moving very slowly so we decided to walk home. On the way back I was seeing giant snowmen throwing snowballs at each other and a sledge pulled by reindeer flying overhead. It seemed to take hours to get back and I was really starting to feel tired, but at the same time I wanted to scream out loud. When I got home I drank a litre of orange juice, lay on my bed and crashed out.

I went to pick Zoe up six hours later. When I got there she was already dressed and waiting to go. The nurse that she had kicked and punched was looking after her. Zoe couldn't remember anything about the night before but, when I told her about it, she couldn't express enough how sorry she was for the unprovoked attack on the nurse. Zoe told me that, when she awoke, she didn't know where she was or if she was dreaming or tripping. When she saw my jacket, she knew I wasn't far away and she was safe.

We went back to her place to begin cleaning up the glass and mess, and she cried when she saw what she'd done to her equipment. She promised herself then that she would never take a trip again, but a little birdie has told me she has actually tripped several times since. Wow! She must be fucking crazy! But this was certainly a night I'll never forget.

DIMINISHED RESPONSIBILITY

I've truly lost count of the number of people I've seen lose it completely due to drugs during the Acid House years. Some bad trips just never end. An example is one guy called Ben, who was a likeable geezer and stood six feet tall with shoulders to match. Somebody introduced him to us and he started coming out now and again with our regular group, which comprised around 30 lads and girls. Wherever we went, we usually had an unlimited guest list so one more person hardly made any difference. Ben had dropped his first tab only a few weeks previously, whereas by now we were virtually professional trippers. I shudder to think now of some of the things we did while monged: not only parachute jumps but dirt-track biking, haunted houses, the works.

One night, Ben bought about twenty purple ohms and started trying to get us all on one with him. We weren't up for it and left the pub early with some of the local talent. Everyone else stayed behind. Ben didn't show his face for a while after that night so we gave his girlfriend a call to check he was OK. She told us he had had a mental breakdown brought on by LSD. The drug had completely deranged his mind and he couldn't even recognise his own girlfriend. She couldn't hack it, and left him.

Ben was in hospital for a few weeks. When he came out, none of his family wanted any friends to visit him so we had to wait for him to contact us. Ben went to Keith's gaff one day to find that no one was home. Ben knocked on Keith's neighbours' door and convinced them that Keith had phoned him and said he was at home in urgent need of assistance. Ben asked if the neighbours would allow him to walk through their house and jump over the garden fence. Keith's place was guarded by Charlie the pit bull terrier – a vicious beast. Somehow, Ben managed to gain the dog's confidence and get into the house.

When Keith returned to an empty house later that evening, the dog had vanished. His neighbour knocked to tell him of his unexpected visitor and Keith drove to Ben's place to see if he had Charlie. Sadly, Ben couldn't remember even going to the house. He wasn't the person we'd known a mere few months before: he'd lost everything, including his girlfriend, house, business... and mind. Keith loved his dog but realised the truth would never be known and he wouldn't see Charlie again. Weeks later, Ben started coming down the pub again but he still clearly wasn't over the LSD effect. He now regarded Keith as a god and wouldn't let me speak to him. If I even went near Keith, Ben would growl and get ready to attack me: he thought I was a devil trying to denounce a god.

One night in the local pub, some of the regular drinkers, who were at least ten years older than us, pulled knives on a friend of ours. Luckily, they never used the weapons, nor even threw a punch: the geezers were just drunk and giving it large. However, later that night a group of my mates were determined to go on a revenge mission on one of the aggressors, who lived across the way.

Ben was with them and, before anybody could say anything, he ran up, booted the door in and went straight into the living room, yelling at the top of his voice. By the time we got in there, the older geezers were shaking with fear, flat against the wall. They'd definitely expected us to come around because there were knives and coshes all over the floor, but now their bottle had gone. They begged us to get Ben away from them and apologised for everything. We dragged Ben away from the scene and went back into the pub. After that night, Ben wasn't seen again for about four years.

When he did come back, thankfully, he was his old, pre-LSD self and hardly remembered a thing. He'd been in various hospitals, but now looked really healthy and well again. He was part of a security team and sweet as a nut. Looking back, I reckon he was lucky: he could easily have spent the rest of his post-Acid life in a straitjacket.

A THATCHED NIGHTMARE

I used to know a charlie dealer who'd bought a thatched cottage in a forest. It was a beautiful gaff set on a private road in the middle of the woods. It had a big garden with a large hedge that went all the way round it and a garage at the bottom. The cottage was the last in a row, and at night it was pitch-black outside due to the lack of street lamps. The dealer's garden had a movement-sensor light that was turned on by anybody entering the garden. It was only triggered off by a figure over four feet tall so wasn't activated by foxes, dogs or any other animals.

I went round to score some gear and, when I arrived, the dealer, Paul, was in the process of chopping some chunky lines out. He and his pals had been sniffing for hours and I didn't need much encouragement to join them in their binge. Time flew by and suddenly it was 4 a.m. and we'd been tooting nonstop for five hours. We were talking a load of garbage, but we were enjoying ourselves. We'd drunk a bottle of Jack Daniels and done a mountain of gear, when, as we sat there laughing and joking, we noticed the light in the garden had come on. We went to investigate and found nobody at all there.

Now, not many people knew where Paul lived and anyone that did know also knew the kind of business he was involved in. They certainly wouldn't just walk into his garden at this time of the morning and not show their face. The boys in Paul's house immediately sprang into action and started loading up the shotguns that were displayed in a cabinet. Then they sat by the window, looking into the dark garden for movement.

I'd only gone to Paul's to buy some gear and suddenly here were all these geezers holding loaded weapons, coked out of their nuts! I said I thought we were being a bit rash and we should calm down a bit because the charlie was making the situation seem a lot worse. We all sat down on the sofa and chopped up another round in silence. By now my nose was seriously clogged up.

Then the light came back on and we jumped up and ran over to the window. There was nobody there but the boys grabbed the shooters and pointed them through the window. After a couple of minutes the light went off again and we stood in silence. Then the geezers legged it into the garden and ran around pointing shotguns at shadows in the darkness. I couldn't believe what was happening! The light came on again as Paul's boys rushed to search all the bushes and the garage, but thankfully they didn't find anyone. After half an hour I made my excuses and left.

I bumped into Paul in the pub a week later and he told me he'd found out who had entered the garden. It turned out to be his brother-in-law, who had come to see him but got spooked by the light and gone back to his car. He'd considered the situation for a while and then returned to the garden and repeated the whole process once again, before getting into his motor and driving off. He had no idea that a gang of paranoid, coked-up geezers had been prowling the garden ready to shoot him – no idea how close he'd come to being killed.

SKID MARKS

It was Saturday night: PARTY TIME! A load of us were round a friend's house before going to a big dance party out in the sticks. Before we left for the gig, we canned a quarter-ounce of sniff. Our mate Dean has only got one leg, he lost the other in an accident, but was mad for life and did his best to have a normal, hectic, eventful lifestyle. He even drove a manual 325i BMW: he'd start the car by pressing the accelerator with his hand, then, once it was mobile, he'd quickly slip it into second gear and continue to change gears with his foot.

Dean loved going out partying and taking untold amounts of drugs. He was an absolute Hoover when it came to sniff. We all went to a party together and dropped a Cali en route. We were heading for a big event held in a series of marquees. It took four hours to get there so by the time we arrived we were off our nut. There were thousands of people in attendance and everyone had a good time: the lights and sound were bang on.

The party got a bit tense now and again because people were taking the piss out of Dean, who was dancing around on one leg. He was pilled up and having a great time and probably didn't even notice the people behind him who couldn't believe what they were seeing and were jumping up and down on one leg. We didn't think this was funny and had a few heated arguments, but we didn't let it spoil our night: we were buzzing hard, mate, and nothing could touch us.

It was raining for most of the night, and at one point it was pouring down and people were still riding the fairground attractions and getting completely soaked in the process (I never could understand that kind of people). After eight hours, the party sadly came to an end and we made our way to the motor, still high on the drugs consumed during the night. Thousands of cars hit the road at once and caused massive tailbacks of traffic, but there was a narrow country lane that went in the opposite direction to the other cars. We decided to go that way and off we went at 50 mph.

My pal Touch had just purchased a brand-new automatic BMW a few days earlier. Our mate Dean was in the passenger seat and three of us were in the back. After a couple of miles we approached some built-up traffic. Touch was slightly out of it and pressed the accelerator and brake at the same time, which caused the vehicle to jerk uncontrollably but not stop. We were twenty yards from skidding into the car in front of us when Dean pulled up the hand brake.

The back of the car came sliding around to the right, did a 180-degree turn straight off the road and landed on its side down a massive ditch. We laughed our bollocks off! Loads of people came running over to the car to find us creased up in laughter. The car was a write-off but we were fine: not even bruised.

We had to squeeze into our pal's motor and drive all the way back to London crammed together in two cars. Touch didn't want the night to end on that note and suggested we go to his place to cane a half-ounce of gear he kept in reserve. We reached his gaff and immediately got out the champagne, Jack Daniels and powder, pouring the contents of the bag on to the glass table.

Touch went to pick up his glass to toast our safe return and somebody knocked over a carton of orange juice, which completely drenched the gear. It was soaked right through and not even a toot could be recovered. Things normally seem to happen in threes so I quit while I was ahead and went home.

PART FOUR

Comebacks and Conclusions

GENESIS REUNION 1992

Probably unwisely, and two years after we'd staged our last party, we tried to make a Genesis comeback in 1992. However, the party landscape had changed a lot since we'd last tried to put on a big event, and almost inevitably our efforts ended in misery and failure. I guess they always say you should never go back.

A close friend of ours owned some shares in a roller-skating rink in north London. It was purpose-built, but also licensed for all-night dance parties. A City venture capitalist whom I knew via a mutual friend and who had heard about the large sums of money to be made in dance parties approached me and offered us the funding to stage two parties at the rink. He gave us a big budget and told us to do whatever we had to do.

When it came to booking the DJs, instead of sticking to the old-school formula, I tried to go with what was happening in the mainstream, which was hardcore music and not the style we played at our original gigs. I booked all the big-name hardcore DJs and two of the biggest MCs, plus state-of-the-art special effects, lighting and a massive stereo sound.

We flooded the market with 100,000 A4 colour flyers and put five different commercials on pirate radio stations and Kiss FM. The gig received loads of press and was featured in an Easter club guide on *TVAM* and in the *Daily Mirror*. We had high expectations and got excellent feedback from clubbers. We even received fanmail congratulating us and wishing us good luck for our comeback gig.

The stage was set and the venue looked the nuts. I remember walking into the centre of the arena. Giant projection screens covered the full length of a side wall. A mate, Pops, designed the artwork for the screens. He had come to our early parties and discovered that he had a talent for designing artwork for flyers, backdrops and projectors. He still creates artwork for a number of companies throughout the UK. It gave me a real rush when I saw our flyer projected on to the screens.

But ticket sales were disappointing: we'd only sold around 1,500 and had 500 guests. Our investor lost over ten grand that night, and we walked away with no wages. That was in return for six solid weeks of hard graft. In retrospect, we should have stuck by our principles and played the music we'd become known for. We'd tried to second-guess the crowd and play what we thought they'd want – hardcore and progressive House. It scared people off, and we learnt our lesson.

However, undeterred, we decided to have one last, desperate blast. Our investor, who wasn't exactly rolling in money, was disappointed with the failure of the previous event but was a staunch geezer and agreed to fund another event. The scheduled date was only four weeks away and we had a lot of hard work to do. Time was ticking away so we printed 100,000 A4 flyers.

I wanted to apply the pressure and keep it on. Everywhere you looked there was a team out promoting Genesis. Our flying crew worked all the hours they could and everyone involved gave it their best. During the second week of the campaign we heard disconcerting news that Raindance were staging an event on the same night as ours. Raindance had a fully licensed site for 5,000 people in Barking, Essex. They were enjoying a very successful run of excellent events. The company were well established and their gig was guaranteed to be rammed to capacity. This was a huge blow to our organisation and left the event in jeopardy. Still, we went all out to promote our gig as the best choice for a stimulating night of enjoyment.

It didn't work. The event was a bigger flop than the first one and we lost another thirteen jib. We were gutted and the investor wasn't too happy either, but he cut his losses as part of the gamble. Again I found myself mentally, physically and spiritually drained of energy. I am often asked if I have any regrets about spending so much money on good times and material possessions. I do have some regrets, but I'd rather regret something I've done than something I haven't. But, having done it all already, that was it for me. I'd had enough.

CONCLUSIONS

Drugs will always play a part in social behaviour. In writing this book I didn't set out to glamorise substance abuse, and by no means to knowingly encourage anyone to take part in any sort of drug ritual. The dangers speak for themselves and the mass-produced synthetic drugs on today's markets are potential killers. Before you give in to the urge of abusing your mind and body and risking death, you have to take a good look at yourself and ask your subconscious some positive questions – beginning with 'Why?'

Ecstasy is the perfect weapon for waging war against mankind. The drug makes you feel highly stimulated and engenders love towards your fellow man. At the same time, it destroys brain tissue at an alarming rate and could create a nation of braindead people who won't be able to think for themselves. This is a thinking person's world: don't let them take away your ability to think clearly and wisely.

The medical profession says that it will take years before all of the long-term, negative side effects caused by Ecstasy become apparent. It's probable that the Class of 88 will be among the first to experience some of these at first hand. There has been an unfortunate number of deaths since the pill started to break through to the mainstream in 1988. One factor agreed by doctors worldwide is that long-term Ecstasy abuse causes irreparable brain damage. They also know that revellers, from the veterans of 1988 to the relative rookies of 1997, will provide research material for the medical fraternity for many years to come.

Hey! I don't mind saying that's scary fucking shit. To think that, in another two or three years, the first real casualties of 1988 will surface as psychiatric patients suffering from a previously unknown brain disorder. Key words for the present time and the future are Love, Trust, Friendship, Unity, Education and Optimism. We have to rebuild the parts of the mind that have not been affected by drug abuse.

I'm not blaming my drug abuse on anybody but myself. I take full responsibility for the joy and pain I have inflicted on myself. We all control our own destinies. In the near future, when the full extent of the damage caused by Ecstasy has been measured through the Class of 88, people will decide to stop slowly killing themselves. But we have to act now. The drugs available today and those to come will drive you towards the same graveyard. Armed with this knowledge, we must regain control of our lives.

If you want my advice, for what it's worth, don't do it. Knowledge and wisdom are fucking power, man. Don't let the oppressors win: keep a strong but flexible drug-free mind. Should we be afraid? I'm scared shitless. The drug may have enhanced my life in different ways but never gave me anything worth losing my mind for. If I knew then what I know now, would I have steered clear of the drug? Well, who knows?

Perhaps at some time in the future our descendants will be able to travel back in time and change life as we know it. But, until such a thing becomes possible, I just hope my future is not going to be viewed from the inside of a padded cell. That would be a sad fucking day, man. By medical calculations, the shit will hit the fan within the next five years and from then on it may well be loony tunes for millions of people.

Of course, my mental state feels almost stable now but the meter is running. We've been suckers, fucking guinea pigs in an experiment that grew out of control. Drug abuse has definitely affected my mind (I'm sure you've already gathered that) in a number of ways and, to be quite honest with you and myself, the symptoms are similar to those predicted by doctors for years.

The most obvious side effect is hallucinations. I have them daily. Never anything too dramatic: they range from movement in shadows to spiders the size of my hand running across the floor and under my bed or chair. Recently, I've also started seeing small flying objects that are not really there. I can't quite make out what they are, because the visions happen too fast.

Depression is another symptom suffered by Ecstasy users. It usually starts on the second day after taking a tablet. Fortunately, through optimism, it is something I have shrugged off so far. I try hard not to succumb to depression, but I can feel its dark presence within my head and could quite easily go down that road.

It's like walking a tightrope between sanity and insanity. Nearly everyone I questioned about the side effects of taking so-called 'designer drugs' told me that they personally know at least one person who has suffered a mental breakdown due to chemical abuse. Some cases are chronic, leaving the user with a deranged mind and possibly committed to a mental institution. Once admitted to hospital, they are given other synthetic drugs to speed them, in theory, towards recovery – or maintain them in a trance-like state. A mental shutdown usually occurs without early warning and can happen to anyone who participates in drug rituals. From the strongest of us to the weakest, we are all vulnerable. Yet, with all this knowledge, we still indulge.

A close friend of mine, Gurkan, was one of the first people in England to die from Ecstasy-related symptoms. He had taken Ecstasy on several occasions, including various excursions to Ibiza. He took a pill while out one night and danced non-stop for six hours, then went home as normal. He didn't wake up the next day. Although we were very unhappy, none of us even thought of giving up the drug. The adrenaline rush of the tablet completely blinded us to the perils of what we were doing.

Because of my views on the world, some of my friends think I'm paranoid. I disagree and say I'm switched on. People try to understand only what's happening on the surface of today's society because it's easier for them to grasp, but once you get into depth – the only way to discover the truth – your opinions are brushed off as the ramblings of someone suffering the symptoms of paranoia. Ever since the Western world's conquerors invaded faraway lands, we have been conditioned to think in certain patterns. In 1997, we encountered numerous numbers of devices every day that maintained and built on this conditioning. It depends on how deep you want to go, and how open-minded you really are, but paranoid? Fuck that shit! I still know what time it is.

I'm trying to repair the damage caused by drug abuse by rebuilding and reconditioning my mind with worldly knowledge, spiritualism, self-healing, internal love and personal development. Writing about my experiences is helping me to confront the past and make way for the future. My inner conflicts will continue for some time to come, and that is the price I am paying for having led such a hedonistic lifestyle. I guess I should think myself lucky to have pulled through thus far with my mind and health intact. The world of drugs is not one I recommend to anyone: it's like playing Russian roulette with your mind, and the minds of those who love and care for you. The experience I gained during those special years is now documented, and I hope it will be of value to the people who read this book and understand where I'm coming from.

Throughout this book I've made what could be regarded as political statements. I'd like to make it clear that I do not support any of the current political parties. My opinions reflect the way I feel and think about such subjects. As the old saying goes, a promise is a comfort to a fool, so what's the point? Most of these parties are the same. Their policies may differ but, at the death of it, all politicians follow the old-school code of honour. It's the same across the globe and nothing less than a miracle will change these firmly established beliefs and deceptions. We need to grow with the rest of the world, not segregate British people by keeping the fallacy of English superiority alive and kicking. Time waits for no one and, the longer we retain a stiff upper lip, the further away a dream of multicultural harmony will drift.

Like most drugs, E was formulated with the intent of aiding the human race in some way. Recently the authorities have been in a state of denial while a plague of badly formed and pressed tablets have flooded the market. People are going to use Ecstasy whatever happens, and a good idea might be for the authorities to interact with those in other countries who have a greater understanding of the subject. In the Netherlands you can find living proof of the interaction between people in the corridors of power and those in the streets. They have realised that the drug cannot be stamped out and are doing their best to prevent a catastrophe by reducing the chances of badly made tablets reaching their commercial market. It doesn't end there, either: at most dance parties you'll find a room or area where punters can test pills they're about to purchase for MDMA content. The procedure provides immediate results in the form of a list of chemicals present in the sample. Germany has followed suit and has decriminalised drug testing at parties, even though Ecstasy is as illegal in both of these countries as it is in the rest of the world. Compromise on the part of their governments allows the drug testing to continue and in turn helps save lives.

Unfortunately, I can't believe Britain would ever adopt such a radical and intelligent scheme, or allow an independent, non-profit organisation to take on this responsibility. I know that would never happen here. My intention is merely to highlight the possible interaction between governments and drug users, and the fact that such liaisons can lead to solutions. A recent survey conducted by MTV, carried out across the continent, revealed startling findings. 44% of people in Europe have tried some kind of mind-altering stimulant in their lifetime. Apparently, a higher proportion of people take Ecstasy in the UK than in any other European state. But, elsewhere, although governments strongly oppose drugs, measures are taken to help combat the threat to human safety.

Obviously testing alone doesn't ensure that your biological system won't reject the drug. No one knows about that until it's too late. And a history of dropping pills for years without harm does not exclude the user from danger as, nowadays, so-called Ecstasy is often pressed with a number of other chemicals thrown into the mix. The government tells us that the Netherlands is the UK's biggest supply source, and I've spoken to people in the 'Dam who tell me the UK is the destination for all the shit tablets. Many buyers in the UK have no desire for clean, quality Es. They simply want a pill that sends them crazy. Pills are manufactured to cause maximum headfuck, and it's not just down to dealers: it's exactly what the current market craves. In 1988 the quest was not for a complete headlock but a mild, light feeling of happiness and empathy. Now it's all about how many you've necked or how intense your buzz is.

Of course the most effective course of action would be for people to stop using the drug, full stop. But, assuming that's unlikely, it is essential that any measures the authorities plan to prevent further death and injury need to be researched and implemented as soon as possible.

Recently it has been reported that an increase in heroin addiction can be attributed to Ecstasy users who have turned to the drug as a way of coming down from E. Are they nuts?!? This theory is bound to add strength to anti-Ecstasy campaigns, and is an exaggeration of the truth – and the biggest load of bollocks I've heard for a while. Here we have two completely separate worlds. A tiny, tiny percentage of Ecstasy users may take smack. But I don't know any who do, and I think it remains a myth.

Epilogue

So eventually, and inevitably, our exciting adventure organising large-scale events had drawn to a close. Looking back on 1989 and the things we went through brings both a smile and a frown to my face. During that period I was kidnapped twice and admitted to hospital on two occasions suffering from yuppie flu (or rather, extreme substance abuse). We had had a few guns stuck in our faces, earned and spent near on a mil and abused a colossal quantity of class As. Unfortunately, we were surrounded by trained killers and had umpteen confrontations with the Old Bill. But we staged some of the most innovative and memorable events in dance-party history. I also met a ton of people, some of whom are my very close friends. Would I do it all again?

No fucking chance.

Appendix

GENESIS PARTY TITLES

Genesis Chapter I: 10 December 1988

Genesis Chapter II: 24 December 1988 – The Struggle
Continues

Genesis Sunset: 31 December 1988 – The Future is
Now

Genesis 1989 Sunset – The Fight goes on

Genesis 1989 Sunset – Against all Odds

Genesis 1989 Sunset – Hedonism

Genesis 1989 Sunset – Strength to Strength

Genesis 1989 – Chapter of Chapters

Genesis 1989 Biology – Together as one

Genesis 1989 – The Empire Strikes Back

Genesis 1989 Pasha – Utopia

Genesis 1989 Pasha – Fight for the Right

Genesis 1989 Pasha – No Surrender

Genesis 1989 Tranquillity – Echoes

Genesis 1989 – Only Love Conquers Hate

Genesis 1989 – Live and Let Live

Genesis 1989 – The Promised Land

Genesis 1989 – See no evil, speak no evil, hear no evil

Genesis 1989 – Fight for the Right

Genesis 1989 Biology – Meopham

Genesis 1989 Biology: 31 December 1989 – Future Power People

Genesis 1989 – (Same Day as Biology)

Freedom to Party Demo: 27 January 1990 – Trafalgar Square

Genesis 1990 – The Warehouse Experience

Genesis 1990 – The Empire Strikes Back

Genesis 1992 – The Awakening Genesis 1992 – The Promised Land